Check Pilot

By the same authors

Flight Briefing for Pilots, Vol. 1
(An Introductory Manual of Flying Training Complete
with Air Instruction)

Flight Briefing for Pilots, Vol. 2
(An Advanced Manual of Flying Training Complete
with Air Instruction)

Flight Briefing for Pilots, Vol. 3
(Radio Aids to Air Navigation)

Flight Briefing for Pilots, Vol. 4
(Associated Ground Subjects)

Flight Emergency Procedures for Pilots

A Guide to Aircraft Ownership

The Tiger Moth Story

Captains and Kings

Flying the VOR

Check Pilot

N. H. Birch AFRAeS

Director Hamilton Birch Aviation Limited
Liveryman of the Guild of Air Pilots and
Air Navigators

A. E. Bramson AFRAeS

Chairman of the Panel of Examiners
Liveryman of the Guild of Air Pilots and
Air Navigators

Pitman Publishing

First published 1973

Reprinted 1976

PITMAN PUBLISHING LTD.
Pitman House, 39 Parker Street, London, WC2B 5PB

PITMAN MEDICAL PUBLISHING CO. LTD.
42 Camden Road, Tunbridge Wells, Kent, TN1 2QD

FOCAL PRESS LTD.
31 Fitzroy Square, London, W1P 6BH

PITMAN PUBLISHING CORPORATION.
6 East 43 Street, New York, NY 10017, U.S.A.

FEARON PUBLISHERS INC.
6 Davis Drive, Belmont, California 94002, U.S.A.

PITMAN PUBLISHING PTY. LTD.
Pitman House, 158 Bouverie Street, Carlton, Victoria 3053,
Australia

PITMAN PUBLISHING
COPP CLARK PUBLISHING
517 Wellington Street West, Toronto, M5V 1G1, Canada

SIR ISAAC PITMAN AND SONS LTD.
Banda Street, P.O. Box 46038, Nairobi, Kenya, East Africa

PITMAN PUBLISHING CO. S.A. (PTY.) LTD.
Craighall Mews, Jan Smuts Avenue, Craighall Park,
Johannesburg 2001, South Africa

© N. H. Birch and A. E. Bramson 1973

ISBN: 0 273 00287 2

Reproduced and printed by photolithography and
bound in Great Britain at The Pitman Press, Bath
G6 G1:18

Preface

One of the problems of learning to fly is that most light aircraft are noisy, expensive and anything but ideal classrooms. It is therefore in the interest of the pilot under training that he should not spend costly time in the air learning what could have been better understood on the ground — at little or no expense. Although a classroom may be the ideal environment in which to learn the various ground subjects it is by no means the only one. Not all flying schools and clubs provide ground school facilities and often the pilot under training can spare only limited time at the airfield. That being so, today's classroom can range from the comfort of the home to the commuter train. As such *Check Pilot* is intended to be your personal examiner. It is suitable for individual or group study.

Some of the questions may appear obvious, others not so readily apparent — while a number will no doubt confuse, but they are all based upon the depth of knowledge required for a Private Pilot's Licence and some of the higher or additional qualifications.

Broadly, the questions are divided between background knowledge and practical application. They are presented in a style similar to that used by the Civil Aviation Authority, the 'multiple-choice' technique. In giving the correct answers our aim has been to provide the reader with a little more than a simple 'right' or 'wrong' because we believe that an incorrect answer points to a lack of understanding, not only of the question but possibly the entire subject. If you select an incorrect answer we tell you why it is wrong and although to this extent *Check Pilot* is a self-contained pilot examiner, we have taken this a stage further by quoting text which should clarify any misunderstanding from within the four volumes of *Flight Briefing for Pilots*. We hope that all pilots, student or qualified, who read this book will find it useful, informative, and dare we suggest, entertaining?

N.H.B.
April, 1973   A.E.B.

v

Contents

Using Check Pilot

Any self-marking system must present even the most honest examinee with certain temptations; the tendency to guess when the correct answer is not known and the urge to see the next answer while checking the one just completed. To obtain full benefit from *Check Pilot* it is suggested that the answers chosen should be listed on paper and only checked at the back of the book when a subject has been completed. To discourage guessing allow one mark for a correct answer and minus one for those that are incorrect. 70% constitutes a minimum pass, 80% a good pass, 90% very good and above 90% excellent.

Flight Briefing for Pilots has been reprinted many times since the first editions and it has therefore been necessary to refer recommended reading to the more recent volumes. The date of the earliest edition that will relate to the page references in this book is as follows —

> Volume 1 — 1971
> Volume 2 — 1973
> Volume 3 — 1970
> Volume 4 — 1970

Check the last date listed overleaf the title page of your existing volumes.

Questions

1. Navigation

1. A line drawn on a topographical map represents:
    (a) A rhumb line,
    (b) A great circle,
    (c) An isogonal.

2. When measuring required track on a topographical map the protractor should be aligned on a meridian:
    (a) Near the beginning of the track,
    (b) Near the destination,
    (c) Near the centre of the track.

3. A track drawn on a Mercator's projection is particularly suitable for:
    (a) Radio navigation,
    (b) Flight over the Poles,
    (c) Long distance navigation.

4. One inch on a 1:500,000 scale map represents:
    (a) Approximately 4 st. m.,
    (b) Approximately 8 st. m.,
    (c) Approximately 8 n. m.

5. Magnetic variation is:
    (a) The difference between True and Compass Heading,
    (b) The difference between Magnetic and Compass Heading,
    (c) The difference between True and Magnetic Heading.

6.   When converting a True Heading to a Magnetic Heading
      variation is applied by:
      (a)   Adding easterly and subtracting westerly variation,
      (b)   Adding westerly and subtracting easterly variation,
      (c)   Adding westerly and subtracting easterly variation
             in the Northern hemisphere and reversing the
             process south of the Equator.

7.   The Required Track is 325°, variation 8°W, deviation
      2°E and calculated drift 8°P. What will be the
      Compass Heading?
      (a)   339° (C),
      (b)   323° (C),
      (c)   327° (C).

8.   After 40 n. m. the aircraft is over a lake 4 n. m. to
      port of a track which measures 120 n. m. How many
      degrees, port or starboard, must the pilot alter
      heading to fly directly to the destination?
      (a)   9°P,
      (b)   9°S,
      (c)   12°S.

9.   After ten minutes flying you are over a bridge 25 n. m.
      down a track measuring 225 n. m. but 3 n. m. to the
      right. What alteration in heading will be necessary to
      regain track in ten minutes?
      (a)   14°P,
      (b)   8°P,
      (c)   14°S.

10.   There are six methods of depicting height above and
      depth below mean sea level on topographical and other
      maps and charts. Can you name them?

11. **What is an isogonal?**
     (a) A broken line surrounding controlled airspace,
     (b) A line on the compass correction card plotting
     .   deviation,
     (c) A line on a map or chart, usually broken, joining
          places of equal magnetic variation.

12. **On a map variation may be shown by the following methods:**
     (a) A correction on each meridian and a statement in
          words,
     (b) Isogonals, diagram, statement in words, compass
          rose,
     (c) A statement in words accompanied by a corrector
          box, a conversion table in the left margin and Air
          Information Circulars issued from time to time.

13. **On the current 1:500,000 series of maps what is the meaning of this sign ⊗ ?**
     (a) A glider site,
     (b) A naval airfield,
     (c) A disused airfield which may be unfit for use.

14. **On the current 1:500,000 series of maps what is the meaning of this sign ▲ ?**
     (a) A compulsory reporting point,
     (b) A non-compulsory reporting point,
     (c) An unlighted obstruction.

15. **While flying over France your track runs across a spot height marked as 600 metres amsl. Assuming you wish to clear the position by 1500 ft at what altitude should you fly?**
     (a) Approximately 3500 ft,
     (b) Approximately 2100 ft,
     (c) Approximately 3950 ft.

16. You plan to fly from Coventry to overhead the White
     Horse at Marlborough, then return to Coventry. On the
     outward flight you are steering 205° (M) to maintain the
     track of 188° (T). The variation is 8°W. What will be
     the Heading for the return flight.
     (a)   351° (M),
     (b)   007° (M),
     (c)   035° (M).

17. The difference between TMG and track required is
     called:
     (a)   Wind effect,
     (b)   Drift,
     (c)   Track error.

18. To assist in estimating TMG in the early stages of a
     map reading exercise the pilot should employ:
     (a)   Five or ten degree fan lines drawn from the point
           of departure either side of track,
     (b)   Time marks,
     (c)   Ten-minute marks along track.

19. When lost a pilot should draw a circle of uncertainty
     on the map and look for features within that area.
     The circle should be:
     (a)   Equal in diameter to the estimated distance flown
           since first uncertain of position,
     (b)   Centred on the DR position using as radius 10% of
           the estimated distance flown since the last pinpoint
           recognized with certainty.
     (c)   Centred on the DR position using as radius 10% of
           the total distance for the flight.

20. **You are flying to a weekend golf meeting. The aircraft is unable to take the golf clubs and your suitcases in the baggage compartment. You should:**
    - (a) Tie the suitcases in the baggage compartment and lay the golf clubs lengthwise along the cabin,
    - (b) Secure the golf clubs in an upright position between the front and rear seats and put the suitcases in the rear baggage compartment.
    - (c) Place the golf clubs in the rear baggage compartment with as much luggage as is permitted and position the remaining suitcase(s) within the cabin.

21. **What preparations can be made before or during flight to assist in revising the ETA?**
    - (a) Divide the track into four equal parts, time the third quarter and revise the ETA when starting the last quarter,
    - (b) Obtain a revised W/V over the radio,
    - (c) Work out distance flown every ten minutes, using computed ground speed and place marks along the track to represent ten minutes flying.

22. **When compiling a flight plan gross errors, e.g. setting the wind or variation in the opposite direction are best avoided by:**
    - (a) Having the flight plan checked by another pilot,
    - (b) Forming the habit of estimating track, drift, distance and time of flight before using the computer,
    - (c) Using a Mercator's Chart.

A Navigational Computer should be used for
the following questions

23.   Calculate Magnetic heading from the following data:
      Track req. 255°; W/V 105/15 kt; TAS 140 kt; variation
      80°W.

      (a)   266° (M),
      (b)   244° (M),
      (c)   260° (M).

24.   You are planning a flight from Biggin Hill to Leicester
      East, a distance of 100 st. m. Track required is 333°
      and the W/V is 290/20 kt. At a TAS of 110 mph the
      aircraft is known to have a fuel consumption of 5 gal/
      hr. Allowing 0.6 gal for the take-off and climb how
      much fuel will be required for the flight.

      (a)   6 gal,
      (b)   5 gal,
      (c)   8 gal.

25.   Convert 120 km to nautical miles.

      (a)   75 n. m.,
      (b)   65 n. m.,
      (c)   80 n. m.

26.   Your IAS is 140 kt and the correction card for that
      speed reads +1 kt. The aircraft is at an altitude of
      8000 ft where the OAT is +5°C. What is your TAS?

      (a)   124 kt,
      (b)   160 kt,
      (c)   157 kt.

27. Your TMG is 045° (T) and the G/S is 135 kt. The air-
    craft is on a Compass Heading of 045°, deviation 2°W;
    variation 8°W, and the TAS is 140 kt. What is the
    wind velocity?
    (a)   128/25 kt,
    (b)   142/22 kt,
    (c)   322/25 kt.

28. Your TAS is 180 kt, the W/V is 160/20 kt and track
    150° (T). What is the True Heading and ground speed?
    (a)   151° and 160 kt,
    (b)   151° and 200 kt,
    (c)   178° and 131 kt.

29. You are flying at an indicated altitude of 10,000 ft. The
    OAT is −10°C. What is your true altitude?
    (a)   10,200 ft,
    (b)   10,550 ft,
    (c)   9800 ft.

30. You are flying a light twin-engine aircraft with a fuel
    capacity of 100 gal. The journey is over a distance of
    725 n. m., the aircraft uses 16 gal/hr while cruising
    at a TAS of 165 kt. On the flight there is an average
    headwind component of 20 kt. Allowing an additional
    5 gal for the take-off and climb how long will the air-
    craft be able to hold over the destination allowing no
    reserves of fuel and assuming that the same power
    setting is used? And how far could you divert in that
    time?
    (a)   56 min = 135 n. m.,
    (b)   2 hr   = 370 n. m.,
    (c)   75 min = 181 n. m.

31.　Your owners manual quotes the fuel capacity of the
aircraft as 50 U.S. gal. How much fuel in Imperial
gallons will it hold?

　　(a)　21.6 Imp. gal,
　　(b)　41.6 Imp. gal,
　　(c)　60　Imp. gal.

32.　On a day when the QNH is 1013 mb you are cleared to
cruise at flight level 75. You plan to climb at a speed of
110 kt when the rate of climb will be 875 ft/min and
at flight level 75 your TAS is 135 kt. How long will it
take to arrive over the destination which is 108 n. m.
away, assuming a 15 kt tailwind component?

　　(a)　40½ min,
　　(b)　42½ min,
　　(c)　44　min.

33.　Your aircraft is refuelled at an airfield in Spain and
you sign for 136 litres. Convert this to Imperial
gallons.

　　(a)　30　Imp. gal,
　　(b)　37½ Imp. gal,
　　(c)　22　Imp. gal.

34.　The maximum authorized weight for the aircraft is
3600 lb. You require 50 gal for the flight. With crew
and passengers but without fuel the aircraft weighs
3080 lb. How much payload remains for baggage
allowing 7.2 lb/gal?

　　(a)　120 lb,
　　(b)　160 lb,
　　(c)　360 lb.

2. Meteorology

1. **Lapse rate is temperature change with height. It changes at a rate of:**
   - (a) $2°F$ per 1000 ft.,
   - (b)   Is dependent on the humidity of the air mass,
   - (c) $2°C$ per 1000 ft.

2. **What is the meaning of the term dew point?**
   - (a)   The humidity in a frontal air mass,
   - (b)   The temperature at which further cooling will cause condensation,
   - (c)   The point at which the air ceases to rise on reaching a similar environmental temperature.

3. **When air rises there is a drop in temperature due to expansion which together with the lapse rate gives a total lapse rate which is known as:**
   - (a)   Adiabatic lapse rate,
   - (b)   Dry adiabatic lapse rate,
   - (c)   Saturated adiabatic lapse rate.

4. **The dry adiabatic lapse rate is:**
   - (a)   A temperature drop of $2°C$ per 1000 ft.,
   - (b)   A temperature drop of $3°C$ per 1000 ft.,
   - (c)   A temperature drop of $2°F$ per 1000 ft.

5.   **Cirrostratus is:**

    (a)   A high-level thin, veil-like cloud,

    (b)   Low-level thin cloud cover in which icing is often present.

    (c)   A high-level shapeless wispy cloud formation.

6.   **Thunder and severe turbulence is associated with:**

    (a)   Cumulonimbus clouds,

    (b)   Nimbostratus clouds,

    (c)   Altocumulus clouds.

7.   **A wind is said to veer when there is:**

    (a)   A clockwise change in direction,

    (b)   A reversal in wind direction.

    (c)   An anti-clockwise change in direction.

8.   **The earth's surface has this effect on lower winds:**

    (a)   It produces smoother flying conditions,

    (b)   It causes a reduction in wind speed, possibly with turbulence,

    (c)   It affects the wind speed but not its direction.

9.   **Radiation fog may form at night under the following conditions:**

    (a)   Clear sky with a normal adiabatic lapse rate and a moist air mass,

    (b)   Clear sky, a gentle wind and a moist air mass,

    (c)   Moist air mass, reasonable cloud cover and a dew point that is easily reached.

10. At ground level the circulation of wind around a depression in the Northern Hemisphere is:
    (a) Clockwise blowing into the centre at approximately 30° to the isobars,
    (b) Anti-clockwise blowing parallel to the isobars,
    (c) Anti-clockwise blowing into the centre at approximately 30° to the isobars.

11. Airframe icing will only occur:
    (a) In cloud below freezing level,
    (b) In cloud at any ambient temperature,
    (c) In any weather conditions below freezing temperature.

12. Airframe icing will affect:
    (a) Effectiveness of controls, stalling speed and airspeed,
    (b) Effectiveness of controls, airspeed but not stalling speed,
    (c) Will decrease the stalling speed and increase the weight.

13. When flying in cloud at an outside air temperature of + 6°C:
    (a) Airframe icing may be expected,
    (b) Carburettor icing may occur,
    (c) There is no risk of airframe or carburettor icing.

14. An aircraft has been left out overnight. It is covered with an icy film which is known as:
    (a) Hoar frost,
    (b) Glazed ice,
    (c) Rime ice.

15. **Flight within a cumulonimbus cloud may entail:**
    - (a) Moderate icing with some precipitation,
    - (b) Severe turbulence, icing, lightning and hail,
    - (c) Little turbulence, no precipitation but a risk of lightning strike.

16. **There is an easterly wind blowing across a range of hills lying North and South. A pilot flying over is likely to notice down draughts on:**
    - (a) The windward side,
    - (b) The leeward side,
    - (c) On both the windward and leeward sides.

17. **The standard barometric pressure is:**
    - (a) 1002.3 mb.,
    - (b) 1003.2 mb.,
    - (c) 1013.2 mb.

18. **After landing an altimeter set on the QFE will always read:**
    - (a) Height above sea level,
    - (b) Zero,
    - (c) Aerodrome elevation above msl.

19. **The QNH is related to:**
    - (a) Altitude,
    - (b) Height,
    - (c) Flight level.

20. **When an aircraft reaches transition altitude the pilot should change his altimeter setting to:**
    - (a) QFE,
    - (b) QNH,
    - (c) The standard setting.

21. Buys Ballot's Law states that in the Northern Hemis-
    phere if you stand with your back to the wind the area
    of lower pressure is:
    (a)   On the right,
    (b)   On the left,
    (c)   Ahead.

22. A change in pressure of 1 mb will alter the reading of
    an altimeter by:
    (a)   30 ft,
    (b)   60 ft,
    (c)   90 ft.

23. When a large anti-cyclone persists during summer in
    the British Isles the weather during the day is likely
    to be:
    (a)   Fine,
    (b)   Low cloud with rain,
    (c)   Thunderstorms.

24. When large cumulus clouds develop which type of
    precipitation may be expected?
    (a)   Drizzle,
    (b)   Heavy showers,
    (c)   Hail.

25. Poor weather conditions exist but a cold front is fore-
    cast to move across the area. When the front has gone
    through the weather will:
    (a)   Improve,
    (b)   Deteriorate,
    (c)   Remain much the same that day.

26. **An aircraft is experiencing starboard drift while flying in the Northern Hemisphere. This indicates that:**
    (a)   The wind is increasing,
    (b)   The aircraft is flying towards an area of low pressure,
    (c)   The aircraft is flying towards an area of high pressure.

27. **Dull weather with continuous drizzle prevails but a warm front is expected to pass through and afterwards flying conditions will:**
    (a)   Be much improved,
    (b)   Include some drizzle and poor visibility,
    (c)   Include a risk of thunderstorms.

28. **When flying in turbulence it is important to:**
    (a)   Increase the airspeed,
    (b)   Decrease the airspeed,
    (c)   Use 10° of flap to lower the stalling speed.

29. **The lines joining positions of equal pressure on a synoptic chart are called:**
    (a)   Isobars,
    (b)   Contour lines,
    (c)   Millibars.

30. **An occluded front is:**
    (a)   A poorly developed inactive cold front,
    (b)   A combination of a cold and warm front,
    (c)   A poorly developed warm front.

31. **The wind was 270/20 kt, which of the following has veered?**

    (a)   240/20 kt,

    (b)   300/20 kt,

    (c)   270/10 kt.

32. **Advection fog is caused by:**

    (a)   Industrial smoke mixing with moist air,

    (b)   A moist air mass being lifted over high ground,

    (c)   A moist air mass drifting over a colder surface.

33. **The station model is found:**

    (a)   On a Synoptic Chart,

    (b)   In a meteorological forecast,

    (c)   On a route forecast.

34. **What are super-cooled water droplets?**

    (a)   Water droplets that form into snow while falling through cloud,

    (b)   Water droplets that remain in the liquid state at below freezing temperature and which freeze on impact with a surface,

    (c)   Water droplets that cause Rime Ice.

35. **A series of closely-spaced isobars on a weather map indicates:**

    (a)   High winds,

    (b)   Low winds,

    (c)   Possibility of a temperature inversion.

3. Aviation Law

1. **The holder of a Student Pilot's Licence may fly solo:**
   - (a) When he is competent to do so,
   - (b) When authorized by a qualified flying instructor,
   - (c) At any time so long as he does not leave the airfield circuit.

2. **A Private Pilot's Licence is valid for:**
   - (a) One year,
   - (b) Three years,
   - (c) Five years.

3. **An aircraft in group 'B' is:**
   - (a) A single-engine aircraft above 12,500 lb mtwa,
   - (b) A single-engine aircraft below 12,500 lb mtwa,
   - (c) A multi-engine aircraft below 12,500 lb mtwa.

4. **The holder of a Private Pilot's Licence may:**
   - (a) Fly passengers for hire and reward, only within the UK,
   - (b) Fly passengers anywhere in the world but not for hire and reward,
   - (c) Fly passengers for hire and reward outside the UK.

5.   In order to maintain a group on a Pilot's Licence with-
     out having to take a flight test the holder must have
     flown an appropriate aircraft within the previous 13
     months for not less than:

     (a) 5 hr,
     (b) 10 hr,
     (c) 10 hr of which 5 hr may be in a simulator.

6.   To obtain a night rating a pilot with the required day
     flying experience must complete at least:

     (a) 5 hr instrument instruction and 5 hr night flying
          under supervision,
     (b) 5 hr instrument instruction and 10 hr night flying
          under supervision,
     (c) 10 hr instrument instruction and 5 hr night flying
          under supervision.

7.   When two aircraft are approaching head on:

     (a) Each shall alter heading to the left,
     (b) The smaller aircraft shall alter heading to the right,
     (c) Each aircraft shall alter heading to the right.

8.   When two aircraft are flying on converging headings:

     (a) The one which has the other on its port side shall
          give way,
     (b) Both shall turn onto diverging headings,
     (c) The one which has the other on its starboard side
          shall give way.

9.   When two aircraft are approaching to land at the same
     time:

     (a) The one which has the greater height must give way
          to the lower aircraft,
     (b) The larger aircraft has right of way,
     (c) The one nearest the runway threshold has right of
          way to land.

10.   **Above 3000 ft outside controlled airspace a pilot must fly within the following weather conditions to remain VMC:**

   (a)   1 mile horizontally and 1000 ft vertically from cloud and 3 n. m. visibility,

   (b)   1 mile horizontally and 1000 ft vertically from cloud and 5 n. m. visibility,

   (c)   1 mile horizontally and 500 ft vertically from cloud and 5 n. m. visibility.

11.   **In the UK flight at night under VFR:**

   (a)   Is not permitted,

   (b)   May be permitted,

   (c)   Is permitted only when the pilot has an instrument rating.

12.   **An area where firing and bombing practice is permanently active by day and night is indicated on a map by:**

   (a)   A pecked or dotted red outline,

   (b)   A solid blue outline,

   (c)   A solid red outline.

13.   **Using the quadrantal rule a pilot making good a magnetic track of 180° would fly:**

   (a)   Odd thousands of feet + 500 ft,

   (b)   Even thousands of feet + 500 ft,

   (c)   Even thousands of feet.

14.   **When flying under VFR, flight separation is the responsibility of:**

   (a)   ATC in the Flight Information Region,

   (b)   The pilot,

   (c)   ATC Service on the frequency being worked.

15. Other than during a landing or take-off, normally an aircraft may not fly close to persons or property. This limit is:

(a) 500 ft,   (b) 1000 ft,   (c) 2000 ft.

16. For flights abroad certain aircraft documents are required. These must include:

(a) C of A, General Declaration, Certificate of Maintenance,

(b) General Declaration, Fuel Carnet, C of A,

(c) C of A, Radio Installation Licence, General Declaration.

17. Two red balls on the signals mast coupled with a double cross in the signals area denotes:

(a) Parachute dropping is in progress,

(b) Instrument meteorological conditions in force,

(c) Glider flying is in progress.

18. An intermittent white beam directed to an aircraft on the ground indicates:

(a) Expedite take-off,

(b) Return to the parking area,

(c) Flight plan has been cancelled.

19. A pilot may file a flight plan at any time but it is mandatory:

(a) If it is intended to fly over the sea,

(b) If radio is not installed in the aircraft,

(c) For flight at night.

20. The UK is divided into the following flight information regions:

(a) London, Preston and Scottish,

(b) London, Midland and Scottish,

(c) Southern, Preston and Northern.

21. Following the malfunction of the undercarriage or flaps
    an R/T call should be prefixed by the words:
    (a)   Mayday-Mayday-Mayday,
    (b)   Security-Security-Security,
    (c)   Pan-Pan-Pan.

22. At night a military aerodrome may be identified by a
    beacon flashing in morse:
    (a)   The airfield letters in green,
    (b)   The airfield letters in red,
    (c)   The airfield letters in white and red.

23. When using a prominent line feature for navigational
    purposes the pilot should:
    (a)   Fly to the right of the feature,
    (b)   Fly overhead the feature,
    (c)   Fly to the left of the feature.

24. Flying instruction for the purpose of gaining a licence
    or rating may be given by:
    (a)   Any pilot with a professional licence,
    (b)   A qualified flying instructor,
    (c)   Any licenced pilot so long as no payment is made.

25. Shortly before a night landing the radio fails and visual
    signals have to be used. The pilot sees a steady red beam
    directed at him from the ground. This means:
    (a)   Land at another aerodrome,
    (b)   Return to your point of take-off,
    (c)   Landing temporarily suspended; wait.

26. **Transition altitude for civil aerodromes is:**
   - (a) 4000 ft amsl,
   - (b) 3000 ft amsl,
   - (c) 3000 ft amsl, except for those situated under the London TMA where it is 4000 ft amsl.

27. **While flying at night you see the green navigation light of another aircraft flying on a similar heading at the same height as your aircraft. It appears to be coming closer. What action would you take?**
   - (a) Hold the present height and heading but be ready to take avoiding action if this is required.
   - (b) Alter heading to starboard,
   - (c) Climb.

28. **The Civil Aviation Authority Accident Investigation Department must be notified when an accident involves:**
   - (a) A forced landing due to engine failure,
   - (b) Damage in a hangar during maintenance,
   - (c) Damage due to a technical defect in the aircraft.

29. **While taxiing back to the parking area you see a vehicle towing an aircraft moving towards your intended path. What action should you take?**
   - (a) Proceed on your present direction since you have right of way,
   - (b) Turn right,
   - (c) Take such avoiding action as is appropriate. The towing vehicle has right of way.

30. **A detailed explanation of aviation law is given in:**
   - (a) The Air Navigation Order and Rules of the Air and ATC Regulations,
   - (b) The General Aviation Flight Guide,
   - (c) Aeronautical Information Circulars.

4. Principles of Flight

1. **When air is induced to flow over an airfoil section:**
   - (a) Pressure is reduced over the top surface,
   - (b) Pressure is increased over the top surface,
   - (c) Pressure is reduced over the top surface and increased below the lower surface.

2. **The centre of pressure is:**
   - (a) The point through which the total effect of lift may be said to act,
   - (b) The point at which maximum drag occurs,
   - (c) The force opposing the centre of gravity.

3. **The angle of attack is:**
   - (a) The angle between the airfoil chord line and the relative airflow,
   - (b) The angle between the relative airflow and the angle of incidence of the wing,
   - (c) A constant determined by the manufacturers.

4. **For a given airspeed lift increases:**
   - (a) As the angle of attack is increased,
   - (b) As the centre of pressure moves forward,
   - (c) As the angle of attack increases and the centre of pressure remains constant.

5. **As the angle of attack is increased:**
- (a) The drag is reduced,
- (b) The drag remains the same if the speed is unchanged,
- (c) The drag is increased.

6. **While performing its stabilizing function the tailplane:**
- (a) Produces no lift,
- (b) Produces lift,
- (c) Produces a correcting force, either up or down.

7. **Directional stability achieved by the fin is also influenced by:**
- (a) The keel surface or area behind the centre of gravity,
- (b) Movement of the centre of pressure,
- (c) Using the 'high wing' design.

8. **If the profile drag at 100 kt were found to be 200 lb, the drag at 200 kt would be:**
- (a) 400 lb,
- (b) 800 lb,
- (c) 1200 lb.

9. **The primary effect of aileron is to cause movement in the rolling plane. The further or secondary effect is:**
- (a) Yaw followed by a spiral dive,
- (b) A skid outwards,
- (c) A nose-up attitude as a result of increased lift on the up-going wing.

10. **The further effect of rudder causes:**
- (a) The aircraft to slip,
- (b) A movement in the rolling plane,
- (c) A movement in the rolling plane followed by a spiral dive.

11. **When the elevator trim tab is set in the up position this will:**
    - (a) Assist the pilot to maintain a nose-up attitude,
    - (b) Will slow down the airflow over the control surface and make it more effective,
    - (c) Assist the pilot to maintain a nose-down attitude.

12. **When an aircraft is flying straight and level at a constant IAS the forces are as follows:**
    - (a) Lift and weight are equal and drag is proportional to the relative airflow,
    - (b) Lift and weight are equal and thrust is proportional to the relative airflow,
    - (c) Lift and weight components are equal and thrust is equal to drag.

13. **When power is adjusted in level flight the slipstream will tend to affect:**
    - (a) The longitudinal stability,
    - (b) Directional stability,
    - (c) Lateral stability.

14. **The maximum rate of climb is achieved at:**
    - (a) A low airspeed and a high power setting,
    - (b) A high airspeed and a high power setting,
    - (c) A compromise between speed and power setting.

15. **Flaps are fitted to an aircraft for the purpose of:**
    - (a) Increasing lift and drag while decreasing the stalling speed,
    - (b) Increasing drag, increasing payload and increasing the stalling angle,
    - (c) Increasing lift, drag and stalling speed.

16. **In addition to the usual benefits, a fowler flap:**
    - (a) Provides a pre-stall buffet,
    - (b) Increases the wing area,
    - (c) May be used to improve the take-off.

17. **In a correctly executed rate 1 turn an aircraft will change direction at:**
    - (a) 360° per min,
    - (b) 2° per sec,
    - (c) 3° per sec.

18. **During a turn total lift balances weight and:**
    - (a) Accelerates the aircraft towards the centre of the turn,
    - (b) Balances weight and does not affect the turn,
    - (c) Has no turning force, the increased lift resulting from the outer wing travelling faster than the inner wing during the turn.

19. **The rate of turn is dependent on:**
    - (a) The airspeed and the angle of bank,
    - (b) The airspeed and the angle of attack,
    - (c) The angle of bank and the power available.

20. **Which of these statements is correct?**
    - (a) Stalling can only occur in certain attitudes,
    - (b) Stalling can occur in almost any attitude,
    - (c) Stalling can only occur when the airspeed is low.

21. **The anti-servo tab on an all-flying tailplane:**
    - (a) Moves in the same direction as the main surface to assist the pilot by removing control loads,
    - (b) Moves in the opposite direction to the main surface to assist the pilot by removing control loads,
    - (c) Moves in the same direction as the main surface to assist the pilot by adding control loads.

22. **During a spin an aircraft is simultaneously:**
    (a)   Pitching up, yawing and rolling,
    (b)   Pitching down, yawing and turning,
    (c)   Pitching up and down, yawing to the accompaniment
           of severe slip towards the spin axis.

23. **To recover from a spin the aircraft must be made to:**
    (a)   Stop rolling with aileron and attain level flight with
           power and elevator.
    (b)   Stop the roll with opposite rudder and attain level
           flight with power and elevator,
    (c)   Stop yawing with opposite rudder, decrease its angle
           of attack with forward elevator, keep straight after
           spinning stops and then resume level flight with
           correct attitude and power.

24. **There are four possible causes of swing during a take-
    off. Those affecting a nosewheel aircraft are:**
    (a)   Torque effect and slipstream effect,
    (b)   Slipstream effect, gyroscopic effect and torque
           effect,
    (c)   Asymmetric blade effect, and torque effect.

25. **During a short take-off, use of the recommended flap
    setting will:**
    (a)   Decrease the take-off run and increase the rate of
           climb,
    (b)   Decrease the take-off run, increase the climb angle
           and probably reduce the rate of climb,
    (c)   Decrease the take-off run without affecting the rate
           of climb.

26. In a turn at a high angle of bank:
- (a) The stalling speed is increased because the angle of attack must be increased,
- (b) The stalling speed is increased because the wing loading is increased,
- (c) The stalling speed is increased because of the inclined lift.

27. Mass balance is fitted to some controls for the purpose of:
- (a) Assisting the pilot to move a heavy control surface,
- (b) Preventing flutter,
- (c) Opposing aerodynamic loads during high 'g' manoeuvres.

28. Lateral stability is built into an aircraft by incorporating the following features:
- (a) High wing, dihedral angle, sweepback, high keel surface,
- (b) Dihedral angle, wash-out, frise ailerons,
- (c) Dihedral angle, wash-out and slats.

29. Some control surfaces are fitted with horn balance for the purpose of:
- (a) Preventing flutter,
- (b) Preventing aileron drag,
- (c) Relieving the pilot of otherwise heavy control loads.

30. On some aircraft small strips are fixed to the leading edges of the wings, close to the fuselage. Their purpose is to:
- (a) Make the aircraft stall more cleanly,
- (b) Prevent a wing dropping at the stall,
- (c) Prevent a wing dropping at the stall and provide a pre-stall warning in the form of a buffet.

31. **When a wing drops during stalling practice the ailerons must not be used to regain lateral level because:**

    (a) The down-going aileron on the wing to be raised would be more fully stalled causing an increase in drag and the risk of a spin,

    (b) At low speeds near the stall the ailerons are not very effective,

    (c) The up-going aileron on the wing to be raised would aggravate the situation.

32. **It is potentially dangerous to commence a gliding turn at a low airspeed because:**

    (a) The risk of stalling is greater in a turn,

    (b) At low speeds there is a risk of aileron reversal,

    (c) There is a risk of an incipient spin developing.

33. **A wing is most efficient when it is flown at an angle of attack of $3\frac{1}{2}°-4°$. This is called:**

    (a) The riggers angle of incidence,

    (b) Minimum drag angle,

    (c) Best lift/drag angle.

34. **Most aircraft have a tailplane. What is its purpose?**

    (a) To provide longitudinal stability,

    (b) To carry the elevators,

    (c) To cater for changes in weight and balance.

35. **What is wheelbarrowing?**

    (a) The tendency to pitch forward during landing due to harsh application of the brakes,

    (b) The tendency during take-off or landing for the aircraft to run along on the nosewheel with the main undercarriage off the ground,

    (c) Instability on the ground due to a faulty nosewheel steering damper.

5. Engines and Propellers

1.   Too weak a fuel/air mixture in a piston engine will
     cause:
     (a)   High fuel consumption and black smoke from the
           exhaust,
     (b)   Loss of fuel pressure,
     (c)   Loss of power, overheating and possibly detonation.

2.   Movement of the pilot's throttle control alters:
     (a)   The main jet,
     (b)   The butterfly valve,
     (c)   The power jet.

3.   Operation of the idle cut-off stops the engine by:
     (a)   Cutting off fuel supply to the slow running jet,
     (b)   Cutting off fuel supply to the carburettor float
           chamber,
     (c)   Earthing the ignition.

4.   With most aero engines in popular use each cylinder
     provides a power stroke:
     (a)   Every two engine revolutions,
     (b)   Every four engine revolutions,
     (c)   Every engine revolution.

5. In a piston engine, in-going mixture and out-going burned gases are controlled by:
    (a) The carburettor heat control,
    (b) The mixture control,
    (c) The inlet and exhaust valves.

6. Two separate ignition systems are fitted to an aero engine for the purpose of:
    (a) Safety in the event of an ignition failure,
    (b) To provide better combustion and safety in the event of an ignition failure,
    (c) To assist engine starting.

7. When the ignition is switched 'off' the magnetos are prevented from generating sparks because:
    (a) The magnetos are earthed to the engine,
    (b) The battery has been switched off,
    (c) The plug leads have been disconnected from the magnetos.

8. In a low-wing monoplane fuel starvation in the event of a failed mechanical fuel pump is safeguarded by:
    (a) Gravity feed,
    (b) The throttle-operated accelerator pump,
    (c) An electric fuel pump.

9. Carburettor icing is of three types:
    (a) Fuel evaporation, impact and throttle ice caused by adiabatic cooling,
    (b) Rime, hoar frost and glazed ice,
    (c) Fuel evaporation, rime and glazed ice.

10. The development of carburettor icing may be recognized by:

    (a)   A gradual decrease in rpm, rough running and eventually complete loss of power,

    (b)   Severe misfiring and fluctuation of the rpm indicator,

    (c)   Sudden loss of power.

11. Before the first flight of the day it is good practice to check the ignition is off, then turn over the engine by hand before starting. Why?

    (a)   To fill the cylinders with mixture and make the engine ready for a cold start,

    (b)   To break the oil film adhesion and so reduce the load on the starter, to check the cylinder compressions and to check for hydraulicing,

    (c)   To prime the oil system.

12. Assuming little or no wind and no met or air traffic restrictions a pilot wishing to fly for maximum range must adopt the following procedure:

    (a)   Select a low altitude and fly at the minimum power setting for level flight,

    (b)   Fly at a high altitude in weak mixture and at the minimum power setting for level flight,

    (c)   Climb to an altitude where full throttle is required to maintain an indicated best L/D speed and weaken the mixture.

13. During take-off nosewheel aircraft have less tendency to swing than tailwheel types because:

    (a)   There is no gyroscopic or asymmetric blade effect from the propeller and nosewheel undercarriages have good directional stability,

    (b)   The pilot has a better view ahead,

    (c)   Slipstream effect cancels torque effect.

14. **When the power setting is altered there is a tendency to yaw due to:**
   - (a) Offset fin or fixed rudder trim,
   - (b) Gyroscopic effect,
   - (c) Slipstream and torque effect.

15. **When an aircraft is fitted with a fixed-pitch propeller a change in airspeed will alter the engine rpm. Why is this?**
   - (a) Because of asymmetric blade effect,
   - (b) Because an increase in airspeed will remove some of the load from the propeller and allow an increase in rpm while a decrease in airspeed has the reverse effect,
   - (c) Because changes in airspeed alter the amount of air passing through the induction system and this affects engine power.

16. **If a coarse-pitch propeller (fixed) ensures a high cruising speed why are they not always fitted to light aircraft?**
   - (a) Because of noise limitations,
   - (b) To avoid high fuel consumption,
   - (c) Because a poor take-off performance results from this type of propeller.

   The following questions relate to constant-speed propellers and multi-engine aircraft

17. **The purpose of fitting a constant-speed propeller is to:**
   - (a) Improve the cruise performance,
   - (b) Provide the most efficient blade angle for all phases of flight,
   - (c) Improve take-off performance.

18. Why do some propellers have three or more blades instead of just two?

   (a)   To absorb high engine powers without resorting to propellers of very large diameter,

   (b)   To provide safety in the event of a blade failure,

   (c)   To increase the airflow over the wing and tail surfaces.

19. The lowest speed at which a light twin-engine aircraft will maintain direction when an engine fails during take-off is:

   (a) V_1 (decision speed),

   (b) V_2 (safety speed),

   (c) V_{mca} (minimum control speed air borne).

20. While turning to the left the starboard engine fails. The aircraft will then:

   (a)   Roll out of the turn,

   (b)   Steepen its angle of bank,

   (c)   Yaw to the right and roll to the left.

21. During asymmetric flight a turn is commenced at a low airspeed. Full rudder proves unable to keep the balance indicator in the centre. The pilot should:

   (a)   Reduce power on the live engine,

   (b)   Move the control wheel forward and increase airspeed,

   (c)   Reduce the angle of bank.

22. During the cruise an engine fails without warning or evidence of serious trouble. The pilot should:

   (a)   Feather immediately,

   (b)   Try to find the cause of failure and re-start the engine before considering feather action,

   (c)   Take immediate engine fire action.

23. **While flying on instruments an engine fails. The turn and slip indicator will show:**

   (a)   A yaw towards the dead engine with a skid in the opposite direction,

   (b)   A yaw towards the live engine with a skid in the same direction,

   (c)   A yaw towards the live engine with a skid in the opposite direction.

24. **The ability to feather the propeller when an engine fails confers these advantages on a multi-engine aircraft:**

   (a)   Reduction of asymmetric drag and the prevention of further damage to the engine.

   (b)   A shorter landing run.

   (c)   Fuel for the dead engine may be transferred to the live engine.

25. **What is the meaning of the term 'zero thrust'?**

   (a)   A power setting used to simulate a feathered engine for the purpose of safe asymmetric training,

   (b)   The power setting achieved at full throttle altitude,

   (c)   A power setting which produces neither thrust nor drag during a descent.

26. **A high outside air temperature has this effect on the engine-out performance of a twin-engine aircraft:**

   (a)   A decrease in single-engine TAS,

   (b)   A decrease in single-engine ceiling,

   (c)   An increase in V_2 (safety speed).

27. Some engines are fitted with a fuel injection unit in place of a carburettor. What is the reason for this?
  (a) To prevent condensation in the fuel system,
  (b) To increase the power of the engine,
  (c) To improve fuel economy and reduce the risk of engine icing.

28. During cruising flight it is noticed that changes of air-speed are accompanied by corresponding alterations in engine rpm on one engine. What is the most likely fault causing this?
  (a) Propeller on affected engine locked in positive fine pitch,
  (b) Low oil pressure on the affected engine,
  (c) Failure of the constant speed unit on the affected engine.

29. At the start of the climb-out after take-off an engine fails. With full rudder direction cannot be maintained. The pilot should:
  (a) Throttle back the live engine,
  (b) Maintain safety speed and assist the rudder with aileron applied in the same direction,
  (c) Abandon the take-off and land ahead.

30. What is the purpose of cross feed?
  (a) A feature of the fuel system designed to prevent an air lock,
  (b) A feature of the fuel system used when checking for water in the tanks,
  (c) A feature of the fuel system for the purpose of making all the fuel carried in the aircraft available to any engine.

6. Instruments

1. Blockage of the static tube or vent will affect the following instruments:
   - (a) ASI, Altimeter and VSI,
   - (b) ASI, Altimeter and Turn Indicator,
   - (c) Altimeter, VSI and Turn Indicator.

2. There is an appreciable elapse of time before the ASI settles to a new airspeed. Why is this?
   - (a) Lag in the instrument,
   - (b) Inertia of the aeroplane,
   - (c) Position error.

3. The difference between IAS and RAS is caused by:
   - (a) Position error,
   - (b) Instrument error,
   - (c) Position and Instrument error.

4. A low air density due to altitude and high temperature will have this effect:
   - (a) Give an increased TAS for any RAS,
   - (b) Give a decreased TAS for any RAS,
   - (c) Give a TAS that is less than RAS.

5. The altimeter obtains its pressure sample from:
   - (a) The static line or static vent,
   - (b) The pressure line,
   - (c) A venturi tube.

6. A sensitive altimeter at low levels is accurate to
    within limits of:
    (a)   + or − 20 ft,
    (b)   + or − 350 ft,
    (c)   +30 or −45 ft.

7. What is the standard ICAN Barometric pressure?
    (a)   1013 mb at mean sea level and 0°C,
    (b)   1013.2 mb at mean sea level and at a temperature
           of +15°C,
    (c)   1013.2 mb at mean sea level and +10°C.

8. You are flying into an area of high pressure. The
    altimeter will:
    (a)   Under read,
    (b)   Over read,
    (c)   Be unaffected.

9. For the purpose of instrument flying high rates of
    descent must be avoided because:
    (a)   The gyro instruments may topple,
    (b)   The aircraft may exceed its V_{ne},
    (c)   The altimeter will lag seriously under conditions
           of high rates of vertical change.

10. You take-off from an airfield with an elevation of 150 ft
    amsl having set the regional QNH of 1012 mb. The
    destination is a non-radio airfield situated on a 600 ft
    hill within the same altimeter setting region. What
    QFE setting should be used for the landing?
    (a)   997 mb,
    (b)   992 mb,
    (c)   1032 mb.

11. For the purpose of calibrating an altimeter a tempera-
     ture of −5°C is assumed at 10,000 ft. What effect will
     a lower temperature have on the instrument at that
     height?
     (a)   It will indicate more than 10,000 ft,
     (b)   It will indicate less than 10,000 ft,
     (c)   No effect because temperature changes are com-
           pensated by a bi-metal link.

12. Within a temperature range of +50°C and −20°C the
     vertical speed indicator is accurate to within limits of:
     (a)   ±200 ft/min,
     (b)   ± 30 ft/min,
     (c)   ±100 ft/min.

13. Viewed face-on a gyroscope is rotating in a clockwise
     direction. Where should you apply a force to make it
     twist to the left (i.e. the right-hand rim will move
     away from you)?
     (a)   Against the top face of the rotating gyro,
     (b)   Against the right face of the rotating gyro,
     (c)   Against the right edge of the gyro, inwards towards
           the centre.

14. The following instruments on the flight panel are gyro
     operated:
     (a)   Artificial horizon, direction indicator and turn and
           slip indicator,
     (b)   Artificial horizon, direction indicator and turn
           indicator,
     (c)   Artificial horizon, direction indicator and slip
           indicator.

15. Why do some gyro instruments topple when the aircraft is placed in an extreme attitude?
    (a)   Because the air supply to the gyro is discontinued,
    (b)   Because the Pendulous Unit is displaced beyond its operating range,
    (c)   Because the Gimbals come up against their limiting stops.

16. Which gyro operated instrument may be relied upon to give factual information during the recovery from a spin (assuming normal toppling limits)?
    (a)   The turn indicator,
    (b)   The slip indicator,
    (c)   The artificial horizon.

17. Before take-off the direction indicator must be synchronized with the magnetic compass. Why is this?
    (a)   Because the gyro may not have reached its correct operating speed,
    (b)   To allow for local magnetic variation,
    (c)   Because a direction indicator has no means of seeking Magnetic North.

18. At regular intervals during flight the direction indicator must be re-set against the magnetic compass. Why is this?
    (a)   Because of mechanical drift,
    (b)   Because of mechanical and apparent drift,
    (c)   Because of turbulence.

19. What feature is incorporated in the direction indicator for the purpose of correcting the effects of apparent drift?
    (a)   A spring attached to one of the gimbals,
    (b)   An adjustable drift nut attached to one of the gimbals,
    (c)   A pendulous unit.

20. **What is the principal advantage of a gyro-magnetic compass over a direction indicator?**
    (a) There are no toppling limits,
    (b) It is suitable for Polar Navigation,
    (c) It incorporates its own north-seeking device and an automatic synchronizing system.

21. **In a vacuum-operated artificial horizon, automatic erection of the gyro is performed by:**
    (a) The pendulous unit,
    (b) A caging device,
    (c) A counter-weight on the horizon bar.

22. **You have just taken-off in a fast aircraft fitted with a vacuum-operated artificial horizon. While climbing straight ahead the instrument will for a short while indicate:**
    (a) A high nose-up attitude,
    (b) A climbing turn to the left,
    (c) A climbing turn to the right.

23. **How is vacuum provided for the gyro-operated instruments?**
    (a) By the static tube,
    (b) By an engine-driven pump or a venturi tube,
    (c) By the static vent.

24. **What is the meaning of the term 'dip' as applied to the magnetic compass?**
    (a) The tendency for the magnet system to tilt during turns,
    (b) The residual deviation present after a compass swing,
    (c) The tendency for the magnet system to be pulled down towards the Earth's magnetic field.

25. **In the Northern Hemisphere what effect will accelera-
     tion and deceleration have on an easterly or westerly
     compass reading?**

     (a)   An apparent turn to South and North respectively,

     (b)   An apparent turn to North and South respectively,

     (c)   No change.

26. **While on a northerly heading within the Southern
     Hemisphere the aircraft is flown left wing low. What
     effect will this have on the compass card?**

     (a)   The south-seeking edge of the compass card will
           swing towards the lower wing,

     (b)   The north-seeking edge of the compass card will
           swing towards the lower wing,

     (c)   No change.

27. **When using a magnetic compass in the Northern
     Hemisphere what is the correct technique for turning
     onto N, S, E, and W?**

     (a)   Roll out of the turn $25^\circ - 30^\circ$ before reaching North,
           $25^\circ - 30^\circ$ after reaching South and $5^\circ - 10^\circ$ before
           reaching East or West.

     (b)   Roll out of the turn $25^\circ - 30^\circ$ after reaching North,
           $25^\circ - 30^\circ$ before reaching South and $5^\circ - 10^\circ$ before
           reaching East or West,

     (c)   Roll out of the turn $25^\circ - 30^\circ$ before reaching North,
           $25^\circ - 30^\circ$ before reaching South, $5^\circ - 10^\circ$ before
           reaching East and $5^\circ - 10^\circ$ after reaching West.

The following questions relate to the use of
instruments

28. Although the required heading is being maintained the
    ball of the slip indicator is over to the left. What
    correction is required to resume balanced flight?

    (a)   Left rudder until the ball centres,
    (b)   Left rudder until the ball centres together with right
          aileron to level the artificial horizon,
    (c)   Right rudder until the ball centres together with
          right aileron to level the artificial horizon.

29. While practicing instrument flying you inadvertently
    place yourself in a position where the instruments
    indicate a balanced rate 4 turn to the left coupled with
    a rapid loss of height and a rapid increase in airspeed.
    What is the aircraft doing?

    (a)   Spinning to the left,
    (b)   In a spiral dive to the left,
    (c)   A steep turn to the left with the pressure tube
          blocked.

30. While climbing at full throttle on instruments you note
    that although the airspeed is correct the rate of climb
    is considerably below normal. What action should you
    take?

    (a)   Adopt a higher nose attitude on the artificial horizon
          and re-trim,
    (b)   Lower the nose slightly and increase the climbing
          speed by approximately 5 kt,
    (c)   Check for carburettor icing.

31. The artificial horizon has become unserviceable during instrument flying. The aircraft enters a steep dive with the airspeed increasing rapidly. During the recovery what indication from the remaining instruments will tell you when the nose is on or near the horizon?

    (a)   When the ASI returns to normal cruising speed,

    (b)   When the ASI stops increasing and the altimeter stabilizes,

    (c)   At the point where the ASI stops increasing and begins to move towards the original cruising speed.

32. What angle of bank should you adopt on the artificial horizon for a rate 1 turn while flying at an IAS of 130 kt?

    (a) 15°,

    (b) 18°,

    (c) 20°.

33. While flying a twin-engine aircraft on instruments there is a sudden turn to the right accompanied by a loss of height and considerable left rudder is required to regain and hold level flight. What is the cause of this and how will it be confirmed by the other instruments?

    (a)   Uneven flow of fuel from the wing tanks which will be confirmed by the fuel gauges,

    (b)   Faulty rudder trim confirmed by the turn and slip indicator,

    (c)   Failure of the starboard engine confirmed when its manifold pressure gauge remains at atmospheric pressure while the throttle is adjusted, a lower airspeed and a gradual lowering of the oil and cylinder-head temperatures.

34. While flying a twin-engine aircraft on instruments the artificial horizon indicates 5° left wing low and this is confirmed by the turn needle. When corrected with right aileron the slip indicator moves out to the right. What is the cause of this?

   (a)   The fixed aileron trim tab requires adjusting,

   (b)   Incorrect rudder trim,

   (c)   The engines are not synchronized.

35. The direction indicator has failed and it is necessary to continue instrument flight using the magnetic compass as the sole heading indicator. When making timed rate 1 turns through a required number of degrees a pilot should:

   (a)   Allow 3° per second and start timing after the correct angle of bank has been attained.

   (b)   Allow 3° per second. Start timing when rolling into the turn and roll out after the required number of seconds have elapsed.

   (c)   Allow 3° per second. Start timing when rolling into the turn and aim to have the wings level again after the required number of seconds have elapsed.

7. Radio Aids to Air Navigation

1. **A QDM is:**
    (a) The magnetic bearing of an aircraft from a station,
    (b) The true bearing of an aircraft in relation to a station,
    (c) The Magnetic heading to be steered by an aircraft to reach a station in conditions of no wind.

2. **A class 'A' bearing is accurate within:**
    (a) $\pm 1^\circ$,
    (b) $\pm 3^\circ$,
    (c) $\pm 2^\circ$.

3. **Other than VHF, radio bearings taken at night are:**
    (a) Less accurate than those taken by day,
    (b) More accurate than those taken by day,
    (c) Unaffected.

4. **If the Magnetic heading is 045° and the radio compass reads 225° the QDM to the beacon is:**
    (a) 180°,
    (b) 270°,
    (c) 225°.

5. **A pilot wishes to track out from an NDB on a heading of 220°. Assuming no wind he will do this when:**
    (a) The radio compass and DI both read 220°,
    (b) The radio compass reads 180°, the DI reads 220°,
    (c) The DI reads 180°, the radio compass reads 220°.

6.   The pilot wishes to maintain a QDM of 270° to the NDB.
      The DI indicates 270° and although the radio compass
      reads 000° this immediately commences to decrease
      because:

      (a)   The wind is from the left,
      (b)   The wind is from the right,
      (c)   The pilot has overflown the beacon.

7.   While joining an NDB holding pattern an aircraft turns
      left from outbound 090° onto inbound 270°. Assuming
      the turn is proceeding correctly what reading should
      be on the radio compass when the DI indicates 300°?

      (a)   300°,
      (b)   270°,
      (c)   330°.

8.   When flying a holding pattern in conditions of cross
      wind the amount of drift should be:

      (a)   Trebled when flying inbound,
      (b)   Trebled when flying outbound,
      (c)   Allowed equally when flying inbound and outbound.

9.   When an EAT of 1230 has been passed by ATC to a
      pilot this indicates that:

      (a)   He is not expected to the airfield facility before
            that time,
      (b)   The descent may not be commenced before that
            time,
      (c)   The landing may not be made before 1230.

10. Having overflown the NDB the pilot turns onto an out-
     bound heading of 090°. The radio compass reads 185°
     and this immediately begins to increase:

     (a)   There is starboard drift,
     (b)   There is port drift,
     (c)   The beacon has not been correctly overflown.

11. When taking up the hold on an NDB above transition
     level the altimeter must be set to:

     (a)   Regional QNH,
     (b)   Airfield QNH,
     (c)   1013.2 mb.

12. A pilot is completing an NDB let-down to the decision
     height when he is instructed to overshoot. He will re-
     set his altimeter to:

     (a)   1013.2 mb,
     (b)   QFE,
     (c)   QNH.

13. To maintain a QDM of 270° with 10° starboard drift
     the DI and radio compass will read:

     (a)   260° and 000°,
     (b)   270° and 010°,
     (c)   260° and 010°.

14. An aircraft flying to an NDB is instructed to leave the
     beacon on a northerly heading. To do this the pilot
     overflies the NDB, turns onto a heading of 015° to gain
     the QDR and when this occurs the radio compass will
     read:

     (a)   165°,
     (b)   180°,
     (c)   195°.

15. After tuning and identifying a VOR beacon it may be used for orientation by rotating the OBS until the deviation needle centres when:

    (a) QDM is read off the main scale with TO showing,
    (b) QDR is read off the main scale with TO showing,
    (c) QDM is read off the main scale with FROM showing.

16. While heading 010° towards a VOR beacon a W/V of 090/15 kt causes the aircraft to drift to port. The VOR indicator would read:

    (a) OBS 010° TO, deviation needle LEFT,
    (b) OBS 010° FROM, deviation needle LEFT,
    (c) OBS 010° TO, deviation needle RIGHT'

17. While using VOR as a let-down aid the pilot selects 170° on the OBS and maintains this QDM for the final approach. After overflying the VOR beacon the deviation needle indications should be:

    (a) Flown in the corrective sense,
    (b) Flown in the reverse sense,
    (c) Ignored when so close to the beacon.

18. An aircraft flying on a heading of 200° crosses the 270° radial of a VOR beacon. Since the OBS is set reading 090° TO the deviation needle is central. If the aircraft continued on its present heading what would be the next VOR indication?

    (a) No change,
    (b) Fly right,
    (c) Fly left.

19. Full deflection of the deviation needle, left or right represents a departure from the selected radial of approximately:

    (a) 2½°.
    (b) 10°,
    (c) 20°.

20. Full deflection of the deviation needle with the 'OFF'
     flag showing indicates that:

     (a)   The VOR beacon is off the air,
     (b)   The VOR receiver has failed,
     (c)   The aircraft is on a radial many degrees removed
           from that selected on the OBS.

21. An aircraft is homing towards a VOR beacon situated
     80 n. m. distant. Within how many miles, port or
     starboard of track indicated may the pilot expect to be?

     (a)   3 n. m.,
     (b)   4 n. m.,
     (c)   2 n. m.

22. A VOR indicator may be used when tuned to an ILS
     frequency. When used to guide an aircraft on the
     approach the OBS should be:

     (a)   Ignored since it has no effect on the deviation needle,
     (b)   Set to the runway QDM,
     (c)   Set to zero.

23. While homing to an airfield a pilot receives successive
     QDMs of 010°, 000° and 357°. This indicates that:

     (a)   The wind is from the left,
     (b)   The wind is from the right,
     (c)   The station has been overflown.

24. At a distance of 3 n. m. from touchdown a pilot on a PPI
     approach should be passing through the following height:

     (a)   1100 ft,
     (b)   950 ft,
     (c)   800 ft.

25. A radar precision approach is normally terminated:
     (a)   At the runway threshold,
     (b)   400 yd from the threshold,
     (c)   At the airfield OCL.

26. The vertical needle on the ILS meter relates to:
     (a)   The glide path,
     (b)   The localizer,
     (c)   Is interelated to glide path and localizer.

27. When flying the QDR of the runway, indications of the
     ILS localizer needle are:
     (a)   In the corrective sense (i.e. needle left-fly left),
     (b)   Inoperative,
     (c)   In the reverse sense.

28. When established on the localizer and approaching the
     ILS glide path the glide path needle will:
     (a)   Give a maximum 'fly up' signal,
     (b)   Give a maximum 'fly down' signal,
     (c)   Remain central until the glide path is intercepted.

29. The ILS outer marker is indicated by:
     (a)   A flashing amber light,
     (b)   A flashing white light,
     (c)   A flashing blue light.

30. An aircraft is above the glide path and to the right of
     the runway centre line. ILS meter indications would
     be:
     (a)   Glide path needle DOWN — Localizer needle LEFT,
     (b)   Glide path needle UP — Localizer needle LEFT,
     (c)   Glide path needle UP — Localizer needle RIGHT.

31. **An aircraft is below the glide path and to the left of runway centre line. ILS meter indications would be:**
    (a) Glide path needle UP — Localizer needle RIGHT,
    (b) Glide path needle DOWN — Localizer needle LEFT,
    (c) Glide path needle UP — Localizer needle LEFT.

32. **When filing an airways flight plan flight levels are:**
    (a) In accordance with the quadrantal rule,
    (b) Related to the direction of the airway,
    (c) Varied according to the traffic density.

33. **What is a fan marker?**
    (a) A position indicator used in conjunction with Loran,
    (b) A VHF beacon transmitting a continuous signal which may be monitored on the airborne radar,
    (c) An airways marker beacon operating on a frequency of 75 MHz which triggers a coded identification signal that may be heard through a headset or identified on the white marker light.

34. **When flying over the facility at a height of 12,000 ft agl the DME indicator will read:**
    (a) 2 n. m.,
    (b) Zero,
    (c) OFF.

35. **At low levels VHF transmissions are of limited range. This is because:**
    (a) The equipment is of low power,
    (b) There is no ground wave,
    (c) There is no sky wave and the ground wave is interrupted by solid objects including the surface of the Earth.

Answers

1. Navigation

1   (b)   A Rhumb Line crosses all meridians at the same angle and an Isogonal is a line joining all places of equal magnetic variation. If you answered (a) or (c) read MAPS AND CHARTS, p. 174 of Vol. 1, also AERONAUTICAL MAPS AND CHARTS on p. 107 of Vol. 4.

2   (c)   Maximum error would occur when measuring track at either end. Remember, the meridians converge towards the Poles. If you answered (a) or (b) read MEASURING TRACK on p. 176 of Vol. 1, and study Fig. 86.

3   (c)   Radio bearings are always Great Circles (shortest distance between two points on a spherical surface). Since lines drawn on a Mercator's Chart are not Great Circles they are therefore not ideal for radio navigation. If you answered (a) or (b) read the paragraph at the top of p. 177, Vol. 1.

4   (b)   The 1:250,000 scale represents approximately 4 statute miles to the inch. If you answered (a) or (c) read SCALE on p. 177 of Vol. 1.

5   (c)   To convert a True Heading into a Compass Heading two corrections are required, one — local magnetic variation and two — deviation caused by the aircraft itself. If you answered (a) or (b) read VARIATION on p. 70 and DEVIATION on p. 72 of Vol. 4.

6   (b)   Remember the little couplet —

"East is least and West is best." This holds true
North and South of the Equator. If you answered
(a) or (c) read ALLOWING FOR VARIATION AND
DEVIATION on p. 73 of Vol. 4.

7   (a)   If you said $323°$ (C) drift was applied in the wrong
             direction and in the case of answer (c) variation
             and deviation were applied in the incorrect sense.
             Think about it.

8   (b)   If the aircraft is to port of track the alteration
             must be in the opposite direction. Read THE ONE
             IN SIXTY RULE, p. 189, Vol. 1, and the explana-
             tion starting at the bottom of p. 104 of Vol. 4.

9   (a) $8°$ port would take you directly to the destination
             but the question asked for a correction to regain
             track in ten minutes, the time already flown. In
             this case the distance to run is irrelevant. If you
             answered (b) or (c) read THE 1-IN-60 RULE,
             bottom of p. 104 until ". . . to his destination, B"
             on p. 105 of Vol. 4 and study Fig. 48.

10   1. Spot Heights (and depths),
             2. Layer Tints,
             3. Contours,
             4. Form Lines,
             5. Hill Shading,
             6. Hachures. If you were unable to remember
             them read RELIEF, bottom of p. 178, Vol. 1 and
             the detailed explanations that follow.

11   (c)   The line surrounding controlled airspace is simply
             a boundary. If you answered (a) or (b) read
             VARIATION on p. 70 to the top of p. 72 in Vol. 4.

12   (b)   Meridians cannot be corrected for magnetic varia-
             tion otherwise it would be impossible to use them
             for determining position. A corrector box is
             fitted to a magnetic compass for the purpose of
             eliminating deviation, the tables in the left margin
             of most maps are for the purpose of converting

feet to metres and Air Information Circulars are
not used for promulgating Variation. If you
answered (a) or (c) read the top of p. 72, Vol. 4.

13   (c)   There is no separate symbol for Naval airfields.
           If you got this wrong study an up-to-date 1:500,000
           map or look at the symbols shown in Fig, 52, p.
           111 of Vol. 4.

14   (a)   If you answered (b) or (c) study an up-to-date
           1:500,000 map or look at the symbols shown in
           Fig. 52 (cont) on p. 112 of Vol. 4.

15   (a)   The first step is to convert 600 metres to feet and
           there is a table printed in the left margin of the
           1:500,000 series maps for the purpose. Alterna-
           tively you could have used the circular slide rule
           on a navigational computer. The method shown on
           p. 100 of Vol. 4 (CONVERTING STATUTE MILES,
           NAUTICAL MILES AND KILOMETRES) and Fig.
           45 are relevant except that for this problem the
           '60' mark on the inner scale should be set against
           the 'KILO/KM-M-LTR' mark on the outer scale
           and the answer read against the mark 'FEET'. In
           this problem the '60' mark represents 600 metres.

16   (b)   The first step must be to determine drift and this
           is only possible when True Track is compared with
           True Heading, or Magnetic Track is compared with
           Magnetic Heading. Answer (a) is the result of
           finding drift by using True Track and Magnetic
           Heading while in answer (c) the correct drift has
           been found and doubled for the return flight, then
           applied in the wrong direction. If you got this
           wrong read MAKING GOOD A RECIPROCAL
           TRACK on p. 107 of Vol. 4 and study Fig. 51.

17   (c)   Wind effect is the difference between Hdg/TAS
           and TMG/Ground Speed while Drift is the angle
           between Heading and TMG. The correct answer
           forms the basis of the '1-in-60' rule. This is an
           important tool of Pilot Navigation and if you

answered (a) or (b) read THE 1-IN-60 RULE, bottom of p. 104 in Vol. 4. The term Track Error appears on the following page.

18 (a) Time Marks or Ten Minute Marks are different names for the same thing and they are used as an aid to anticipating pinpoints. If you answered (b) or (c) read from "Within the first five or ten minutes . . ." on p. 188 to the end of the first paragraph on p. 189 of Vol. 1 and study Fig. 92.

19 (b) When lost the error will have occurred after the last pinpoint was recognized with certainty. If you answered (a) or (c) read ACTION TO BE TAKEN WHEN LOST on p. 193 of Vol. 1.

20 (c) Modern golf clubs have steel shafts and they must be kept well away from the magnetic compass. If you answered (a) or (b) read DEVIATION on p. 72 of Vol. 4.

21 (a) A revised W/V would involve handling the computer while flying and working out a new Heading and Ground Speed using a wind that is in any case only estimated. Ten Minute Marks may be an aid to map reading but they are of little assistance in revising the ETA. If you answered (b) or (c) read TIME on p. 190 of Vol. 1.

22 (b) Unless he is experienced the other pilot may be a less proficient navigator than you and a Mercator's Chart is usually unsuited for pilot navigation. If you answered (a) or (c) read the first four paragraphs of THE FLIGHT PLAN on p. 191 of Vol. 1.

23 (c) An answer like 266° (M) would indicate that you have applied the wind in the opposite direction while (b) is a case of Variation applied in the wrong sense. If you selected (a) or (b) read HOW TO FIND Hdg(T) and G/S (and DRIFT) on p. 91 of Vol. 4, study Figs. 40 and 41 — and don't forget, "East is least and West is best" (ALLOWING FOR

VARIATION AND DEVIATION, p. 73, Vol. 4).

24   (a)   Here is a case where the aircraft's speed is quoted
           in mph (no doubt because the ASI is calibrated that
           way) so it is therefore more convenient to measure
           distances in statute miles. This means converting
           the wind speed from 20 kt to 23 mph, giving a G/S
           of 92 mph and an elapse time of 65 min. If you
           made an error on the computer read CALCULATING
           TIME AND DISTANCE ON FUEL REMAINING,
           p. 100 of Vol. 4.

25   (b)   If you said 75 that is the answer in statute miles
           while answer (c) means you have set 120 against
           'WEIGHT IN KILOGRAMMES' instead of the
           'KILO/KM-M-LTR' on the outer scale of the
           computer. Read CONVERTING STATUTE MILES,
           NAUTICAL MILES AND KILOMETRES on p. 100
           of Vol. 4 and study Fig. 45.

26   (b)   Answer (a) will occur if you use the outer scale
           for RAS and the inner scale to find TAS. The two
           scales should in fact be used the other way round.
           You will arrive at answer (c) if -5°C is set on the
           computer instead of $+5^{\circ}$C. If you got this wrong
           read AIRSPEED INDICATOR AND ALTIMETER
           CORRECTIONS, on p. 102 of Vol. 4, and study
           Fig. 46.

27   (c)   Answer (a) is the result of applying Variation and
           Deviation incorrectly. "East is least and West is
           best" only applies when converting from True to
           Magnetic and from Magnetic to Compass. Here is
           a case where we know the Compass Heading and
           must convert to True so the 2°W and 8°W must be
           applied in the opposite sense. If you got this
           wrong read HOW TO FIND W/V WHEN Tr. AND
           G/S ARE KNOWN on p. 93 of Vol. 4, and study
           Figs. 42 and 43.

28   (a)   Answer (b) will result when the wind is applied in
           the reverse direction and (c) is the product of two

errors; using the TAS as Track and the Track as
TAS. If you answered (b) or (c) read HOW TO
FIND Hdg(T) AND G/S (AND DRIFT) on p. 91 of
Vol. 4, and study Figs. 40 and 41.

29 (c) (a) is the result of reading from the outer to the
inner scale on the circular slide rule while (b) is
the answer that will occur with an OAT of $+10^{\circ}$C
whereas the question said that the temperature
was -10°C. If you chose (a) or (b) read ALTI-
METER CORRECTIONS on p. 104 of Vol. 4.

30 (a) This is a simple matter of converting time at 16
gal/hr into total gallons used, after allowing an
extra 5 gal for the take-off and climb. If you
answered (b) or (c) read CALCULATING TIME
AND DISTANCE ON FUEL REMAINING on p. 100
of Vol. 4.

31 (b) If you align 50 against the 'U.S. GAL' mark on the
outer scale of the computer the answer may be read
against the 'IMP GAL' position.

32 (c) Here is a problem embracing slight variations on
some of the previous exercises and calling for a
little common sense. The first step should be to
jot down the Ground Speed in the climb and in the
cruise, in this case 125 kt and 150 kt respectively
allowing for the 15 kt tailwind. Next determine
the proportion of the flight at each speed. This is
decided for you by the time required to reach
Flight Level 75 (on this day corresponding to an
altitude of 7500 ft). To find time of climb set 1
(actually 10) on the inner scale against 875 on the
outer scale. Look for 75 (your flight level) on the
inner scale and read off 8½ min for the climb. The
remainder of the problem is a simple matter of
time and distance. An 8½ min climb at 125 kt will
cover a distance of 17.6 n. m. leaving 90.4 n. m.
to complete the journey which at 150 kt means
another 35½ min.

33   (a)   This is a straightforward conversion using the
             relevant marks on the computer's outer edge, i.e.
             'KILO/KM-M-LTR' for the litres to be converted
             and 'IMP GAL' for the answer.

34   (b)   To find the weight of 50 gal at 7.2 lb/gal, set 1
             (actually 10) on the inner scale against 7.2 on the
             outer scale, then find the weight against 50 on the
             inner scale which is 360 lb. Add this weight of
             fuel to the 3080 lb, subtract from the maximum
             authorized weight of 3600 lb and the result is the
             weight available for baggage.

2. Meteorology

Answer   Comments and Study References

1   (c)   These days the °F scale is rarely used in aviation.
            If you answered (a) or (b) read TEMPERATURE
            on p. 31 of Vol. 4.

2   (b)   An understanding of the meaning of DEW POINT
            is important because this is the starting point of
            all fog and cloud formations. If you answered
            (a) or (c) read HUMIDITY on p. 32 of Vol. 4.

3   (b)   It is only after the Dew Point has been reached
            and cloud has begun to form that the air is satura-
            ted with moisture. If you answered (a) or (c) read
            TEMPERATURE on p. 31 to the top of p. 32 in
            Vol. 4.

4   (b)   Answer (a) is the lapse rate with height without
            the influence of further cooling due to expanding,
            rising air. If you answered (a) or (c) read the
            first sentence at the top of p. 32 in Vol. 4.

5   (a)   Any cloud name beginning with 'Cirrus' or 'Cirro'
            is high while 'Stratus' (at any level) denotes a
            layer formation. If you answered (b) or (c) study
            CLOUDS (bottom of p. 32 to the top of p. 34 in
            Vol. 4) and look at the cloud photographs between
            p. 36 and 37.

6   (a)   The deciding factor in this question is the word
            thunder and that can only mean one type of cloud.
            If you answered (b) or (c) read the top paragraph
            on p. 34 of Vol. 4.

7 (a) If you have difficulty in remembering whether 'veer' means clockwise or anti-clockwise there can be no mistaking the direction of the opposite term 'back' since this is the same as putting the clock back or anti-clockwise. If you answered (b) or (c) read VEERING AND BACKING on p. 34 of Vol. 4.

8 (b) While much will depend upon the nature of the ground even a smooth surface is bound to retard the wind, perhaps cause eddies and therefore turbulent flying conditions. This is explained under SURFACE WINDS on pp. 34-35 of Vol. 4. Answer (c) is also incorrect because a reduction in wind speed due to ground friction alters the balance of the Geostropic wind. Read from "On a weather map . . ." to ". . . Geostrophic wind (Fig. 12)" on p. 40 of Vol. 4, also study Figs. 11 and 12.

9 (b) Fog is not caused by ascending air therefore adiabatic cooling is not involved and answer (a) is incorrect. Cloud cover would have the effect of retaining heat below its base and so prevent the drop in temperature required for radiation fog. If you answered (a) or (c) read RADIATION FOG on p. 35 of Vol. 4.

10 (c) This is another case of having to remember which is clockwise and which anti-clockwise. Those who have difficulty may care to remember 'we may have a low aunty but at least we have a high clock'. Answer (b) would be correct for winds at 1500 ft and higher. This is explained on p. 40 of Vol. 4 ("On a weather map . . ." to ". . . Geostrophic wind (Fig. 12)").

11 (c) One of the mistaken beliefs of aviation is that airframe icing will only occur in cloud. If you answered (a) or (b) read ICE ACCRETION on p. 54 to the top of p. 55 in Vol. 4.

12   (a)   A decreased stalling speed as a result of increased
             weight is an aerodynamic contradiction (read
             FACTORS AFFECTING THE STALL, item (a) on
             p. 96 of Vol. 1). If you answered (b) or (c) read
             PRINCIPAL CAUSE OF GLAZED ICE on p. 55 of
             Vol. 4.

13   (b)   Airframe icing will not occur at a temperature of
             +6°C. While no pilot in this day and age should be
             in doubt about this question if you did answer (a)
             or (c) as a matter of urgency read CARBURETTOR
             ICING on p. 39 of Vol. 2 and CARBURETTOR HEAT
             CONTROL on p. 26 of Vol. 4.

14   (c)   This is a case of understanding how the various
             types of airframe ice are formed. If you answered
             (a) or (b) read ICE ACCRETION on pp. 54-57 in
             Vol. 4.

15   (b)   Clouds of considerable vertical extent are always
             associated with turbulence and the developed
             cumulus or cumulonimbus represents an extreme
             case. Therefore answer (c) must be incorrect
             while (a) makes no mention of turbulence or the
             likelihood of hail. Read THUNDERSTORMS on
             p. 60 of Vol. 4.

16   (b)   If you answered (a) or (c) read from 'The behaviour
             of wind . . ." on p. 58 of Vol. 4 to ". . . conditions
             of strong wind" at the top of p. 59 and study Fig.
             23.

17   (c)   If you answered (a) or (b) 'no comment' but read
             THE ALTIMETER, bottom of p. 61 to the end of
             the first paragraph on p. 62 of Vol. 4.

18   (b)   If you answered (a) or (c) read ALTIMETER
             SETTINGS on pp. 62-64 of Vol. 4.

19   (a)   If you answered (b) or (c) read ALTIMETER
             SETTINGS on pp. 62-64.

20   (c)   If you answered (a) or (b) read STANDARD

ALTIMETER SETTING on p. 64 of Vol. 4.

21   (b)   If you can remember that answer (c) is wrong it
             is then a matter of deciding if the area of low
             pressure is to the left or right. To help you
             decide read HORIZONTAL PRESSURE CHANGES
             AND THE ALTIMETER, page 64 to the top of
             p. 68 and study Fig. 27.

22   (a)   If you answered (b) or (c) read the last paragraph
             on p. 65 of Vol. 4.

23   (a)   Other than a tendency for haze generally a high-
             pressure system is always associated with good
             weather (see ANTICYCLONE OR HIGH on p. 43
             of Vol. 4).

24   (b)   The larger the rain drop the more vertically
             developed will be the cloud of origin and this
             rules out answer (a). Hail is more usually
             associated with cumulonimbus clouds. If you
             answered (a) or (c) read PRECIPITATION on
             p. 38 of Vol. 4.

25   (a)   Unless there is another depression moving in
             behind the cold front its passing must bring a
             period of much improved weather. This is best
             understood by studying the two-dimension illus-
             tration (Fig. 17) on p. 47 of Vol. 4.

26   (b)   To answer this question Buys Ballot's Law must
             be understood. This is explained in the section
             headed HORIZONTAL PRESSURE CHANGES AND
             THE ALTIMETER, page 64 to the top of p. 68.
             Also study Fig. 27 on p. 67.

27   (b)   The passing of a warm front heralds the Warm
             Sector. If you are not clear about flying con-
             ditions within this part of a low-pressure system
             read THE WARM FRONT on p. 46 of Vol. 4.
             Also study Fig. 17 on p. 47.

28 (b) Increasing the airspeed while flying in turbulent conditions can only add to the strains imposed on the airframe while lowering flap without reducing IAS below the Flap Limiting Speed could likewise cause airframe damage. If you answered (a) or (c) read from "To reduce the risk of structural damage . . ." at the top of p. 58 to the end of paragraph (b) in Vol. 4.

29 (a) Contour lines are used to illustrate shape on maps and charts. If you answered (b) or (c) read the third paragraph on p. 40 of Vol. 4.

30 (b) If you answered (a) or (c) read the last paragraph of THE COLD FRONT on p. 48 of Vol. 4 and study Fig. 18.

31 (b) If you answered (a) or (c) read VEERING AND BACKING on p. 34 of Vol. 4.

32 (c) Smoke mixing with moist air results in what the popular press call 'smog' or industrial haze. A moist air mass that is cooled through being lifted over high ground causes Orographic Cloud, not fog. If you answered (a) or (b) read ADVECTION FOG on p. 37 of Vol. 4.

33 (a) While the Station Model is used by a meteorologist to draw a Synoptic Chart on which to base his forecasts it is not part of a pilot's route or other forecast. If you answered (b) or (c) read from "The position of each reporting station . . ." on p. 50 of Vol. 4 to the top of p. 52 and study Fig. 19.

34 (b) Water droplets that form into snow are unlikely to present the pilot with any hazard whereas super-cooled water droplets often will. If you answered (a) or (c) read PRINCIPAL CAUSE OF GLAZED ICE on p. 55 of Vol. 4. Also study Fig. 21.

35   (a)   Isobars that are closely spaced may be regarded
             as contour lines. On a map closely spaced contour
             lines denote a steep rise (or fall) in surface level.
             Likewise closely spaced isobars on a weather map
             indicate a steep fall or rise in pressure. If you
             answered (b) or (c) read the third paragraph on
             p. 40 of Vol. 4.

3. Aviation Law

Answer		Comments and Study Reference

1   (b)   Answer (a) is partly correct but it should make clear that a flying instructor is responsible for saying when the student is competent. Alternative (c) cannot be right. This would mean that a student pilot would be unable to practice cross country flying. If you answered (a) or (c) read STUDENT AND PRIVATE PILOTS' LICENCES, pp. 119-121 in Vol. 4.

2   (c)   If you answered (a) or (b) read the last paragraph on p. 120 in Vol. 4.

3   (c)   If you answered (a) or (b) see the first paragraph on p. 121 in Vol. 4.

4   (b)   If you answered (a) or (c) read the sentence above the heading COMMERCIAL PILOTS' LICENCE on p. 121 of Vol. 4.

5   (a)   If you answered (b) or (c) read from "In order to maintain . . ." on p. 121 of Vol. 4 to the end of that paragraph.

6   (a)   If you answered (b) or (c) read NIGHT RATING on p. 125 in Vol. 4.

7   (c)   Answer (b) would be impossible in practice. How could one tell if a similar aircraft was larger or smaller from a distance of perhaps several miles? If you answered (a) or (b) read No. 3 under RIGHT OF WAY IN THE AIR on p. 128, Vol. 4 and study Fig. 54.

8   (c)   If you answered (a) or (b) read No. 2 under RIGHT
             OF WAY IN THE AIR on p. 128, Vol. 4 and study
             Fig. 53.

9   (a)   If you answered (b) or (c) read No. 7 at the top of
             p. 130 in Vol. 4.

10   (b)   The question relates to flights above 3000 ft. The
             rule allows pilots to remain VMC over the top of
             cloud. If you answered (a) or (c) read RELATED
             WEATHER CONDITIONS, p. 131 in Vol. 4.

11   (b)   In the UK all night flying is classed as IFR and
             this is mentioned under 2 (iii) on p. 131 of Vol. 4.
             The following proviso (iv) on that page explains
             that pilots without an instrument rating may obtain
             a Special VFR Clearance, conditions permitting.

12   (c)   If you answered (a) or (b) read RESTRICTED
             AREAS on p. 138 of Vol. 4.

13   (c)   Since the Quadrantal Rule may often be the only
             means of ensuring separation from other aircraft
             while flying in marginal weather outside controlled
             airspace it is vital that the procedure should be
             fully understood. If you answered (a) or (b) as a
             matter of urgency read FLIGHTS OUTSIDE CON-
             TROLLED AIRSPACE AND THE QUADRANTAL
             RULE, pp. 139-140 and study Fig. 60 in Vol. 4.
             There is a misprint in the caption to that illustra-
             tion and also in the statement that follows (up to
             1970 edition). The Quadrantal Rule extends from
             3000 ft to 25,000 ft (not 29,000) when the high-
             level semi-circular rules apply. This is explained at
             the bottom of p. 140.

14   (b)   In-flight separation is a responsibility that is
             shared between pilots and the Air Traffic Control
             Service. The dividing line is contingent upon the
             type of flight plan and the weather. This aspect
             of aviation law touches on one of the foundation
             stones of safety in the air. If you answered (a)

or (c) read AIR TRAFFIC CONTROL on p. 130 of
Vol. 4, also 2(i) under RELATED WEATHER
CONDITIONS on the following page.

15   (a)   If you answered (b) or (c) read LOW FLYING pp.
            141-142.

16   (c)   When flying abroad the Certificate of Maintenance
            is, perhaps surprisingly, not required. While a
            Fuel Carnet is very useful it is not a legal docu-
            ment. If you answered (a) or (b) read CARRIAGE
            OF CERTIFICATES AND LICENCES on p. 148 of
            Vol. 4.

17   (c)   While most aircraft these days have good radio,
            ground signals are still important. If you
            answered (a) or (b) study the signals illustrated
            in the front and rear covers of Vol. 4.

18   (b)   Like the previous question, light signals may
            appear irrelevant in these days of good radio
            communications but even the best equipment has
            been known to fail. Then the ability to recognize
            light and other signals could do much to ease an
            otherwise difficult situation. If you answered (a)
            or (c) read VISUAL SIGNALS on pp. 143-144 of
            Vol. 4.

19   (c)   While for most non-airways flights a pilot is not
            required to file a flight plan he should neverthe-
            less book out. This is in his own interest. If
            you answered (a) or (b) read THE FLIGHT PLAN
            on p. 147 of Vol. 4.

20   (a)   Answer (b) is the name of a now defunct railway
            company and (c) is also incorrect. If you made
            the wrong selection read CONTROLLED AIR-
            SPACE to the bottom of p. 132 in Vol. 4 and study
            Fig. 57.

21   (c)   If you answered (a) or (b) read EMERGENCY on
            p. 155 of Vol. 4.

22   (b)   If you answered (a) or (c) read BEACONS on p.
             143 of Vol. 4.

23   (a)   If you fly overhead the feature it will most likely
             remain out of view and alternative (c) would pre-
             sent a hazard to pilots who knew the answer to
             this question and obeyed the rule. This is
             explained under No. 5 of RIGHTS OF WAY IN THE
             AIR, p. 128 of Vol. 4. (Also see Fig. 56.)

24   (b)   No instruction given to a student by any non-
             qualified instructor pilot, whatever his experience
             is admissible for the purpose of gaining a licence
             or rating, even when no payment is involved. If
             you answered (a) or (c) read FLYING INSTRUC-
             TORS' RATINGS on p. 125 of Vol. 4.

25   (c)   If you answered (a) or (b) read VISUAL SIGNALS
             on pp. 143-144 in Vol. 4.

26   (c)   If you answered (a) or (b) read TRANSITION
             ALTITUDE on p. 20 of Vol. 3.

27   (a)   This is a case where another aircraft is converg-
             ing with its starboard wingtip on your port side
             (the position of aircraft navigation lights is
             explained on p. 143 of Vol. 4). While No. 2
             under RIGHTS OF WAY IN THE AIR p. 128, Vol.
             4 shows that the other aircraft must alter heading
             this does not absolve you from taking evasive
             action should this prove necessary.

28   (c)   If you answered (a) or (b) read AIRCRAFT
             ACCIDENTS on p. 146 of Vol. 4.

29   (c)   An aircraft being towed by a vehicle is an un-
             wieldy combination and must surely warrant
             every consideration. If you answered (a) or (b)
             read RIGHT OF WAY ON THE GROUND on p.
             130 of Vol. 4.

30   (a)   While much information, mainly of an operational
             and facility nature is contained in The General
             Aviation Flight Guide, the fountain head is that
             mentioned in answer (a). If you selected (b) or
             (c) read from "The foregoing information . . ."
             on p. 148 of Vol. 4 to the end of p. 149.

4. Principles of Flight

1 (c) Answer (a) is only part of the story and if (b)
      were true aeroplanes would always remain firmly
      on the ground. If you answered (a) or (b) read
      the first three paragraphs under BEHAVIOUR OF
      AN AIRFOIL SECTION, p. 15 of Vol. 1 and study
      Figs. 5 and 6.

2 (a) The Centre of Pressure refers to Lift, therefore
      answer (b) is incorrect. Since it is not a force
      but the point through which total lift is exerted,
      (c) is also incorrect. If you chose either answer
      read from "Lift is generated . . .", bottom of p.
      15 to the top of p. 17 in Vol. 1, also study Figs.
      9 and 10.

3 (a) The Angle of Incidence is measured between the
      fuselage datum line and the airfoil chord line.
      While this is fixed by the manufacturer, Angle
      of Attack is under the control of the pilot. If you
      answered (b) or (c) read the whole of BEHAVIOUR
      OF AN AIRFOIL SECTION (p. 15 to the top of p.
      20 of Vol. 1) and study the diagrams referred to
      in the text.

4 (a) Forward movement of the Centre of Pressure is
      a by-product of increased lift, not its cause. For
      this reason answers (b) and (c) are incorrect and
      if you selected either of these read ANGLE OF
      ATTACK on p. 19 of Vol. 1 and study Fig. 12.

5 (c) If drag reduced as we increased the angle of

attack the IAS would **increase** as the stick was
moved back. Answer (b) is also incorrect because
you cannot increase the angle of attack and have
the airspeed remain unchanged. If you answered
(a) or (b) read from the bottom paragraph on p. 17
of Vol. 1 to ". . . usually occurs at $3\frac{1}{2}°$-$4°$ (Fig. 12)"
on p. 19 and study Fig. 12.

6   (c)   If you answered (a) or (b) read THE AEROPLANE,
p. 21 of Vol. 1 to ". . . function of the tailplane
clear" on p. 24 and study all the diagrams men-
tioned in the text.

7   (a)   Movement of the Centre of Pressure in fact causes
longitudinal **instability** while the 'high wing' layout
is sometimes used to create **lateral** stability. If
you answered (b) or (c) read the paragraph
commencing "Notwithstanding the addition . . .",
half way down p. 24 in Vol. 1 and study Fig. 21.

8   (b)   Aerodynamic forces vary according to the square
of the speed (V^2 law). If you answered (a) or (c)
read PROFILE DRAG, pp. 1-2 of Vol. 2.

9   (a)   If you answered (b) or (c) read FURTHER EFFECTS
OF AILERON on p. 42 of Vol. 1 and study Fig. 30.

10   (c)   If you answered (a) or (b) read FURTHER EFFECTS
OF RUDDER on p. 42 of Vol. 1 and study Fig. 31.

11   (c)   When the trim tab moves UP it displaces the elevator DOWN and this in turn will raise the tail
and lower the nose. If you answered (a) perhaps
you were a little confused, while answer (b)
indicates a serious lack of knowledge on this par-
ticular subject. In either case read THE TRIMM-
ING CONTROLS, p. 43 to the top of p. 46 and
study Fig. 33.

12   (c)   All aerodynamic forces — not just drag — are proportional to the relative airflow and thrust is
proportional to the power output of the engine.

If you answered (a) or (b) read the DESCRIPTION
to the bottom of p. 54 in Vol. 1 and study Fig. 35.

13   (b)   While to a minor extent power changes will affect
             longitudinal and lateral stability the main distur-
             bance is directional. If you answered (a) or (c)
             read from the last line on p. 54 of Vol. 1 to the
             end of the first paragraph on p. 56, also study
             Fig. 36.

14   (a)   A high airspeed must reduce the rate of climb.
             Answer (c) is incorrect because maximum power
             is required for maximum rate of climb. If you
             answered (b) or (c) read DESCRIPTION, p. 60 to
             the top of p. 62 in Vol. 1 and study Fig. 38.

15   (a)   Slats, not Flaps, increase the stalling angle of
             the basic airfoil and Flaps do not increase the
             stalling speed as suggested in answer (c). Read
             THE LANDING APPROACH, pp. 66-67 in Vol. 1.

16   (b)   Flaps are not fitted to provide a pre-stall buffet
             and Fowler Flaps are not unique in offering
             improved take-off performance when the correct
             technique is used. However they are unusual in
             improving lifting power partly by increasing the
             wing area. This is shown in Fig. 42, p. 67 of
             Vol. 1.

17   (c)   If you answered (a) or (b) read from "the number
             of degrees . . ." to the bottom of the page (p. 77)
             in Vol. 1 and study Fig. 47.

18   (a)   While it is true that extra lift is produced by the
             outer (faster) wing during a turn the effect of this
             is a tendency to overbank. If you answered (b)
             or (c) read DESCRIPTION on p. 75 of Vol. 1 to
             ". . . than that desired" on p. 77 and study Fig.
             46.

19   (a)   Angle of attack affects airspeed and power avail-
             able is the factor limiting the steepness of the

turn. If you answered (b) or (c) read from the last line on p. 77 of Vol. 1 to the end of the first paragraph on p. 78.

20 (b) Other than in a steep dive stalling can occur in any attitude and a 'g' manoeuvre capable of considerably increasing the wing loading could cause a stall at almost any speed within the range of the aircraft. If you answered (a) or (c) read FACTORS AFFECTING THE STALL on p. 96 of Vol. 1 and the paragraph above that heading. Also study Fig. 59.

21 (c) A Balance Tab moves in the opposite direction to the main control (see BALANCE TABS on p. 18 of Vol. 2 and study Fig. 12 in that book). If you answered (a) or (b) read from "Not all aircraft . . ." on p. 46 to the end of the paragraph in Vol. 1 and study Fig. 34.

22 (a) While some aircraft tend to oscillate in the pitching plane during a spin it should be remembered that the manoeuvre takes the form of a low speed unbalanced spiral dive. Therefore the nose must be pitching towards the centre or axis of the spin i.e. UP in relation to the pilot. If you answered (b) or (c) read DESCRIPTION on p. 102 to the top of p. 104 in Vol. 1.

23 (c) During a spin the rolling motion is caused by the yaw so there is no point in trying to prevent it with aileron, particularly since the down-going wing will be fully stalled. The recovery must entail removing the cause of the spin which is Yaw, and Yaw is controlled with rudder. If you answered (a) or (b) as a matter of urgency read the whole of Chapter 12 (p. 102, Vol. 1) including the FLIGHT PRACTICE.

24 (a) Gyroscopic Effect and Asymmetric Blade Effect are only of consequence when taking-off in a tailwheel aircraft. If you answered (b) or (c)

read NOSEWHEEL AND TAILWHEEL AIRCRAFT
to the bottom of that page (p. 109 in Vol. 1).

25   (b)   Using the correct short take-off technique and
             climbing at the recommended flaps-down speed,
             the climb gradient will improve, although only
             slightly in the case of most low-powered light
             aircraft. However the rate of climb usually
             suffers, therefore answer (c) is incorrect. If
             you selected answer (a) or (c) read USE OF FLAP
             DURING TAKE-OFF on p. 112 of Vol. 1 and study
             Fig. 66.

26   (b)   The stalling angle of an airfoil remains the same
             in level or banked flight and while answer (c) is
             partly true it is misleading because it is the turn-
             ing force element of the inclined lift that increases
             the wing loading. A similar situation exists when
             pulling out of a dive or pulling too tightly around
             a loop. In each case the wing loading is increased
             although there is no bank angle. If you answered
             (a) or (c) read DESCRIPTION pp. 142-46 in Vol.
             1 and study the illustrations mentioned in the text.

27   (b)   Answer (a) refers to Aerodynamic Balance. If
             you selected (a) or (c) read FLUTTER on p. 20
             of Vol. 2 and study Fig. 16.

28   (a)   Wash-out is the reduction in angle of incidence
             towards the wing tip which is built into an air-
             craft for the purpose of preventing the tendency
             for a wing to drop at the stall. Frise Ailerons
             are designed to reduce aileron drag (p. 22 and
             Fig. 17 in Vol. 2) and Slats have nothing to do
             with stability (you can read about them on p. 98
             of Vol. 1). If you answered (b) or (c) read
             LATERAL STABILITY on p. 12 of Vol. 2 and
             study Figs. 8, 9 and 10.

29   (c)   Flutter is caused by a lack of structural rigidity,
             the penalty of having to reduce airframe weight
             to a minimum, (see FLUTTER, p. 20 and Fig.

16 in Vol. 2). Aileron Drag has no connection
with Horn Balance (read AILERON DRAG, p. 22
and study Fig. 17 in Vol. 2). If you got it wrong
read HORN BALANCE, p. 17 in Vol. 2 and study
Fig. 11.

30   (c)   If you answered (a) or (b) read from "Conversely
it is sometimes . . ." to ". . . pre-stall warning
buffet" on p. 99 of Vol. 1.

31   (a)   In effect, lowering an aileron increases the angle
of attack and even at low airspeeds this is bound
to encourage the full development of a stall.
Answer (c) is also incorrect because the up-going
aileron is in fact on the wing that has to be **lowered**
during stall recovery. Read THE FULLY DEVEL-
OPED STALL, p. 97 to the end of the first paragraph on p. 98 in Vol. 1.

32   (c)   While it is true that the higher wing loading in a
turn will increase the stalling speed this is of
little consequence unless the bank angle is steep
and 'g' is applied. However a stall during even a
gentle gliding turn is likely to develop into an
incipient spin. If you answered (a) or (b) read
the first paragraph under CLIMBING AND
DESCENDING TURNS on p. 78 of Vol. 1.

33   (c)   The Riggers Angle of Incidence is not an angle of
attack and drag could be reduced by flying at a
smaller angle than $3\frac{1}{2}°$-$4°$. If you answered (a)
or (b) read from the top of p. 18 in Vol. 1 to the
end of the first paragraph on p. 19 and study Fig.
12.

34   (a)   While the tailplane does compensate for changes
in weight and balance it also compensates for
movements of the centre of pressure, therefore
answer (c) is incomplete. Answer (b) should
not be taken too seriously. If you answered (b)
or (c) read THE AEROPLANE, p. 21 to ". . . of
the tailplane clear" on p. 24 of Vol. 1 and study.

Figs. 15, 16, 17, 18, 19 and 20.

35   (b)   When one is fitted a faulty nosewheel steering
           damper will allow the assembly to vibrate or
           'shimmy'. This is not Wheelbarrowing. If you
           answered (a) or (c) read TAKING-OFF, NOSE-
           WHEEL TECHNIQUE, pp. 110-11 in Vol. 1.

5. Engines and Propellers

Answer		Comments and Study References
1	(c)	If you answered (a) or (b) read p. 2, Vol. 4.
2	(b)	Engine speed is controlled by the Butterfly Valve. If you answered (a) or (c) read p. 3, Vol. 4.
3	(a)	The Idle Cut-off has nothing to do with the ignition system. If you answered (b) or (c) read p. 26, Vol. 4.
4	(a)	It may be called a Four-Stroke Engine but there are two strokes to every revolution (one up and one down). If you answered (b) or (c) read FEEDING THE MIXTURE TO THE ENGINE on p. 3, Vol. 4 and study Fig. 5.
5	(c)	If you answered (a) or (b) read p. 7, Vol. 4 and study Fig. 5.
6	(b)	(a) is only part of the answer and (c) is wrong. In fact many engines are started on one magneto. If you answered (a) or (c) read DUAL IGNITION on p. 22, Vol. 4.
7	(a)	The battery has no connection with magneto ignition and the plug leads are connected to the magnetos all the time. If you answered (b) or (c) read IGNITION SWITCHES on p. 24, Vol. 4.
8	(c)	Gravity feed will only work when the tanks are mounted above the engine as in a high-wing monoplane. The throttle-operated accelerator pump

would be of little help because it too also depends on the carburettor for its supply of fuel. If you answered (a) or (b) read FUEL BOOSTER PUMP on p. 27 of Vol. 4.

9   (a)   Rime, Hoar Frost and Glazed Ice are types of airframe icing. If you answered (b) or (c) read CARBURETTOR ICING, p. 39, Vol. 2 and CARBURETTOR HEAT CONTROL on p. 26, Vol. 4.

10   (a)   Severe misfiring is almost invariably due to ignition trouble and sudden power loss will most likely be caused by some form of fuel starvation. If you answered (b) or (c) read CARBURETTOR ICING on p. 39, Vol. 2.

11   (b)   Cylinders are made ready for starting either with the primer or the throttle operated accelerator pump. The oil system is self-priming. If you answered (a) or (c) read the first paragraph, p. 33, Vol. 1 and ELECTRIC STARTER on p. 28 of Vol. 4.

12   (c)   You fly 'low and slow' for maximum endurance (i.e. maximum time in the air). If you answered (a) or (b) read FLYING FOR RANGE, p. 36, Vol. 2.

13   (a)   A competent pilot can keep straight even when the view ahead is reduced by a tail down/nose up attitude. Slipstream, torque and for that matter all four propeller effects act in the same direction. If you answered (b) or (c) read THE TRI-CYCLE UNDERCARRIAGE, p. 51, Vol. 1, NOSEWHEEL AND TAILWHEEL AIRCRAFT, p. 109, Vol. 1 and THE PROPELLER DURING TAKE-OFF, p. 51, Vol. 2.

14   (c)   Offset Fin and fixed rudder trim are devices intended to provide feet-off balanced flight at cruising power. Gyroscopic Effect will only

occur when the propellers plane of rotation is altered. If you answered (a) or (b) read p. 54 to the top of p. 56 in Vol. 1, also SLIPSTREAM EFFECT and TORQUE EFFECT on p. 51 of Vol. 2.

15   (b)   Answer (a) is incorrect because asymmetric blade effect only occurs when the propeller shaft is inclined relative to the aircraft's path along the ground or through the air. In any case it will have no direct effect on engine rpm. Answer (c) while partly true would not produce a noticeable change in rpm. If you answered (a) or (c) read ENGINE SPEED INDICATOR, p. 59, Vol. 1, also from last paragraph p. 41 to ". . . propeller blade (Fig. 26)" on p. 46, Vol. 2. Study Fig. 26.

16   (c)   A coarse pitch propeller would in fact run at lower rpm, thus reducing both noise level and fuel consumption. It also prevents the engine developing maximum power for take-off. If you answered (a) or (b) read from 'During take-off . . .' on p. 43 of Vol. 2, study Fig. 26 and read CONVERSION OF POWER INTO THRUST, p. 19, Vol. 4.

17   (b)   Answer (a) is only part of the story and so is answer (c). If you selected either of these read PROPELLERS on p. 48 of Vol. 2 and study Figs. 26, 27 and 28. Also read CONVERSION OF POWER INTO THRUST, p. 19, Vol. 4.

18   (a)   A blade failure on any propeller would almost certainly cause sufficient vibration to remove the engine from its mountings. If you answered (b) or (c) read bottom of p. 46 to ". . . the advent of jet propulsion". (Half-way down p. 48).

19   (c)   Decision Speed (V_1) is the maximum speed on the ground that will allow the pilot to abandon the take-off and remain on the runway. It does not apply to aircraft of less than 12,500 lb maximum weight.

The figure quoted for V_2 allows a safety margin over Minimum Control Speed which is what the term implies. If you answered (a) or (b) read FAILURE OF AN ENGINE DURING TAKE-OFF on p. 225 of Vol. 2.

20   (a)   When an engine fails in straight flight or during turns the aircraft will always roll towards the dead engine. Since roll and yaw are interrelated answer (c) would be quite impossible. If you chose (b) or (c) read ENGINE FAILURE DURING TURNS, p. 224 in Vol. 2, and study Fig. 90.

21   (c)   Reducing power during a low-speed turn is bad flying technique in any aeroplane and in any case the loss of height that will follow such action may present an additional danger. Similarly answer (b) involves a height loss that may be unacceptable at the time. If you chose (a) or (b) read ASYM-METRIC-POWERED MEDIUM AND STEEP TURNS on p. 224 of Vol. 2.

22   (b)   Why feather the engine when the cause of failure may be cured simply by switching on the fuel booster pump? If you selected answer (c) read the question again. Remember it said there was 'no evidence of serious trouble'. If you got it wrong read FAILURE OF AN ENGINE DURING CRUISING FLIGHT on p. 220 of Vol. 2.

23   (a)   When an engine fails yaw is always towards the dead engine usually accompanied by a skid towards the live engine. If you answered (b) or (c) read INSTRUMENT INDICATIONS on p. 223 of Vol. 2.

24   (a)   By reducing windmilling drag a feathered pro-peller may in fact lengthen the landing run. Cross-feed may be used without having to feather the failed engine, there being no connection between the two functions. If you answered (b) or (c) read FEATHERING PROPELLERS on p. 48 of Vol. 2.

25 (a) Full Throttle Altitude is usually associated with
         flying for maximum range and Thrust is certainly
         not 'zero' under these conditions. If you answered
         (b) or (c) read PRACTICING ASYMMETRIC LAND-
         ING AND OVERSHOOT PROCEDURES on p. 231
         of Vol. 2.

26 (b) A high outside air temperature has the effect of
         increasing the TAS for any given IAS and the speed
         quoted for V_2 is in any case an IAS. If you
         answered (a) or (c) read OUTSIDE AIR TEMPER-
         ATURE, p. 220, Vol. 2.

27 (c) Condensation is most likely to occur in the fuel
         tanks and a fuel injection system cannot prevent
         this. Power output is not materially affected by
         choice of induction, i.e. carburettor or fuel
         injection. If you answered (a) or (b) read the
         paragraph dealing with DIRECT INJECTION on
         p. 27 of Vol. 4.

28 (c) In the case of (a) and (b) the most likely result
         would be an overspeeding propeller due to
         excessive fine pitch. If you gave either of these
         answers read CONSTANT-SPEED PROPELLER
         FAULTS on p. 50 of Vol. 2.

29 (b) The question makes clear that the engine failure
         has occurred at the beginning of the climb-out
         so there may be insufficient height at that stage
         to throttle back the live engine. However by that
         phase of the take-off and climb V_2 should have
         been attained so that a landing ahead will not be
         necessary. At any time while in asymmetric
         flight aileron may be used to assist rudder. This
         is mentioned at the top of p. 215, Vol. 2 ('Under
         certain conditions . . .'). If you answered (a) or
         (c) read ENGINE FAILURE AFTER TAKE-OFF
         WHEN SAFETY SPEED HAS BEEN REACHED
         on p. 228 of Vol. 2.

30   (c)   Vents are provided to prevent air locks and fuel
             strainers are incorporated for the purpose of
             detecting water in the tanks. If you answered (a)
             or (b) read FUEL SYSTEMS on p. 63 of Vol. 2.

6. Instruments

Answer   Comments and Study References

1   (a)   Like the other gyro instruments the turn needle
              will, if not electrically driven be powered by a
              vacuum source. Only the pressure-operated
              instruments will be affected by a pressure/static
              blockage. If you answered (b) or (c) read
              PRESSURE-OPERATED INSTRUMENTS on p. 75
              of Vol. 2.

2   (b)   For all practical purposes there is no lag in an
              ASI and Position Error will only affect the
              accuracy of its readings. If you answered (a) or
              (c) read ERRORS, bottom of p. 75 in Vol. 2.

3   (c)   While (a) and (b) are both partly correct they do
              not individually give the complete answer. If
              you got it wrong read from the top of p. 78 in
              Vol. 2.

4   (a)   Both height (i.e. reduced atmospheric pressure)
              and high temperatures for that height will reduce
              the air density and the greater the reduction the
              larger the increase in TAS for any RAS.
              If you answered (b) or (c) study the table at the
              bottom of p. 78 in Vol. 4 and try some examples
              on a computer.

5   (a)   Venturi Tubes are more common on older types
              of aircraft. They are used to supply vacuum
              to the gyro-operated instruments and there is no
              connection between the venturi tube and the
              pressure instruments. If you answered (b) or
              (c) read THE ALTIMETER on p. 79 of Vol. 2.

6   (c)   Although the instrument will register height
            changes of 20 ft or even less an altimeter is not
            accurate to these limits. If you answered (a) or
            (b) read ACCURACY on p. 82 of Vol. 2.

7   (b)   If you answered (a) or (c) read BAROMETRIC
            ERROR on p. 81 of Vol. 2.

8   (a)   The thing to remember here is that high pressure
            is safe and low pressure is unsafe because the
            aircraft is lower than indicated. If you answered
            (b) or (c) read BAROMETRIC ERROR on p. 81 of
            Vol. 2.

9   (c)   It would have to be a very steep dive for either
            (a) or (b) to apply. If you chose either of these
            alternatives read LAG ERROR on p. 82 of Vol. 2.

10   (b)   Since the destination airfield is within the same
            Altimeter Setting Region the QNH already set
            will apply. On landing the altimeter would read
            600 ft (the destination elevation amsl) at the
            existing setting. Therefore the instrument must
            be wound down 600 ÷ 30 = 20 mb to obtain zero
            on landing (QFE). If you answered (a) or (c) read
            DETERMINING CIRCUIT HEIGHT AT THE
            DESTINATION AERODROME, p. 68 in Vol. 4.

11   (b)   The bi-metal link or strip will only compensate
            for expansion and contraction of the components
            within the altimeter. It cannot correct changes
            in the atmosphere due to temperature. If you
            answered (a) or (c) read TEMPERATURE ERROR
            on p. 81 of Vol. 2 and ALTIMETER CORREC-
            TIONS on p. 104 of Vol. 4.

12   (a)   The rather large errors that may be present at
            quite small rates of ascent or descent are the
            prime reason why the VSI should be regarded
            as an approximate guide to vertical change. If
            you answered (b) or (c) read ERRORS on p. 83
            to the top of p. 84 in Vol. 2.

13   (a)   By applying a force towards the centre (from the
             circumference) a gyro would simply move in that
             direction. To answer this question you must
             understand the '90° Rule'. If you answered (b) or
             (c) read from "The second important property of
             a gyroscope . . ." on p. 86 of Vol. 2, and study
             Fig. 41.

14   (b)   The Slip Indicator usually takes the form of a
             damped pendulum or ball. If you answered (a) or
             (c) read PRINCIPLE on p. 88 of Vol. 2, also
             SLIP INDICATOR on p. 90.

15   (c)   Although in some instruments the air supply to
             the gyro buckets may discontinue during an
             extreme attitude normally these attitudes are
             only held for a few seconds. In that time the
             gyro will continue to spin under its own momen-
             tum. The Pendulous Unit is peculiar to the
             Artificial Horizon only and in any case its function
             is not to topple the instrument.

16   (a)   Although the Slip Indicator will give useful infor-
             mation during a spin recovery it is not a gyro
             instrument. Only certain designs of Artificial
             Horizon have complete freedom of movement in
             roll and pitch. Others will have toppled during
             the spin and so be unable to assist during the
             recovery. If you answered (b) or (c) read THE
             TURN AND SLIP INDICATOR on p. 88 to the top
             of p. 91 in Vol. 2, and study Fig. 43.

17   (c)   Magnetic Variation is irrelevant because the DI
             is used to steer Magnetic Headings, therefore it
             must be synchronized with the Magnetic Compass.
             If you answered (a) or (b) read FUNCTION on p.
             92 of Vol. 2.

18   (b)   While alternatives (a) and (c) are in themselves
             correct they only give part of the answer.
             Furthermore the effects of turbulence are a
             contributing factor of Mechanical Drift. If you

chose (a) or (c) read ERRORS, MECHANICAL DRIFT and APPARENT DRIFT on pp. 94 and 95 of Vol. 2.

19 (b) Spring damped gimbals are used in Turn Indicators and the Pendulous Unit is part of the Artificial Horizon. If you answered (a) or (c) read APPARENT DRIFT on p. 95 of Vol. 2.

20 (c) No heading indicator which relies upon a magnetic system is suitable for Polar navigation (see Fig. 52 and read from the beginning of the first sentence on p. 84 of Vol. 1 to the words ". . . becomes impracticable"). If you answered (a) or (b) read HEADING INDICATORS on p. 96 of Vol. 2.

21 (a) While some Artificial Horizons do incorporate a caging device that will also erect the gyro not al! instruments have this and in any case the question asked how the function was performed **automatically**. There is a counterweight on the horizon bar but its purpose it to balance that assembly. If you answered (b) or (c) study Figs. 46 and 47 in Vol. 2 and read from the top of p. 100 to ". . . vacuum pump or venturi tube", on p. 101.

22 (c) A climbing turn to the left would be indicated by an electrically driven Artificial Horizon where gyro rotation is in the opposite direction to vacuum-operated instruments. If you answered (a) or (b) read ERRORS, ACCELERATION and DECELERATION on pp. 101 and 102 of Vol. 2.

23 (b) The Static Tube or Vent is for the pressure-operated instruments (ASI, VSI and Altimeter). If you answered (a) or (c) read the last paragraph on p. 87 of Vol. 2.

24 (c) While it is true that the magnet system will tilt in relation to the horizontal during turns this is caused by the normal turning forces and not Dip. Residual Deviation after a Compass Swing is

called Coefficient A and this again has nothing to do with Dip. If you answered (a) or (b) read from the last paragraph on p. 83 of Vol. 1 to ". . . the magnetic compass becomes impracticable", on p. 84. Also study Figs. 52 and 53.

25 (b) While there would be no change in reading while flying on a northerly or southerly heading, acceleration and deceleration error is most pronounced on east and west. If you answered (a) or (c) read from "On easterly or westerly . . ." to ". . . return to its true heading" on p. 85 of Vol. 1, and study Fig. 55.

26 (a) The thing to note in this question is that it relates to flight within the Southern hemisphere, but north or south of the Equator the compass will be affected while flying wing low unless it is on an easterly or westerly heading. If you answered (b) or (c) read from the last paragraph on p. 84 to ". . . Fig. 54 explains" on p. 85 of Vol. 1, study Fig. 54 and read the third paragraph on p. 87.

27 (a) Answer (b) would apply when flying in the southern hemisphere and (c) never at all. If you got this wrong read from "To overcome these errors . . ." at the bottom of p. 85 to ". . . able to settle down" on p. 87 of Vol. 1.

28 (b) An out-of-balance indication without turn must be the result of crossed controls and reference to the Artificial Horizon in this case would confirm that the left wing is down. Answer (a) would convert the situation into a left turn while (b) would increase the slip to the left. If you answered (a) or (c) read STRAIGHT AND LEVEL FLIGHT, CLIMBING AND DESCENDING on p. 91 of Vol. 2, also item (c) in the Air Exercise on p. 123.

29 (b) If the pressure tube became blocked there would be no airspeed indication while the

Altimeter and the VSI would remain unaffected.
Answer (a) means that you cannot recognize the
difference between a spin and a spiral dive; in
this case as a matter of urgency read THE SPIN
ON THE LIMITED PANEL on p. 118 of Vol. 2,
and study Fig. 55.

30   (c)   The question makes clear that you are climbing
at the correct speed, therefore any departure
from this, higher or lower can only result in a
reduction of the existing rate of climb. Provided
the aircraft is not overloaded or flying under 'hot-
and-high' conditions an abnormally low rate of
climb is most likely caused by reduced engine
power. While there can be many causes of this
carburettor icing is one that is under the control
of the pilot.

31   (c)   Answer (a) will place the aircraft in a high nose-
up attitude and this will be followed by a rapid
decrease in airspeed. While (b) is recommended
by some instructors it is complex and not very
effective due to altimeter lag. If you answered
(a) or (b) read RECOVERY FROM A DIVE on p.
135 of Vol. 2.

32   (c)   It is a commonly held but mistaken belief that all
Rate 1 turns, irrespective of IAS are at 15° angle
of bank. If you answered (a) or (b) read OPERA-
TION IN FLIGHT on p. 103 of Vol. 2.

33   (c)   While answer (a) or (b) could cause the aircraft
to turn they are not likely to do so suddenly or
require correcting with a lot of rudder. If you
answered (a) or (b) read INSTRUMENT FLYING
IN MULTI-ENGINED AIRCRAFT, p. 118 of Vol. 2.

34   (b)   The fact that the aircraft is out of balance when
the wings are held level must point to incorrect
rudder trim. In this case it should be adjusted
to hold on sufficient right rudder to centre the
ball. Remember, the ball is controlled with

rudder. Aileron trim would have been the cause
had the ball remained in the centre when the wings
were level. If you answered (a) or (c) read
STRAIGHT AND LEVEL FLIGHT, CLIMBING
AND DESCENDING on p. 91 of Vol. 2.

35 (b) Answer (a) is incorrect and incomplete since
there is no mention of when to stop the turn and
(c) will overshoot the required heading. If you
answered (a) or (c) read TURNING on p. 115 of
Vol. 2.

7. Radio Aids to Air Navigation

Answer		Comments and Study References

1   (c)   A magnetic bearing FROM a station is a QDR. If you answered (a) or (b) read DESCRIPTION on p. 54 of Vol. 3 to the first two lines on p. 55.

2   (c)   If you answered (a) or (b) read ACCURACY to the bottom of p. 58 in Vol. 4.

3   (a)   All radio transmissions affected by reflection are in varying degrees subject to 'night effect'. If you answered (b) or (c) read from the bottom of p. 56 in Vol. 3 to ''. . . for direction finding purposes (Fig. 20)'' on p. 57 and study Fig. 20.

4   (b)   If you answered (a) or (c) read the first paragraph under the heading of RADIO MAGNETIC INDICATOR (RMI) on p. 71 of Vol. 3 and study Fig. 24.

5   (b)   The question made clear that there was no wind, therefore you can only track on a Heading of 220° when the DI reads 220°. When the NDB is directly behind the aircraft the Radio Compass is bound to read 180°. If you answered (a) or (c) read FLYING OUTBOUND FROM A BEACON on p. 83 of Vol. 3 and study Fig. 32.

6   (a)   In questions of this kind always remember that the Radio Compass needle points to the beacon at all times, indicating the progress of the aircraft relative to the transmitter. If you answered (b) or (c) study Fig. 31 on p. 82 of Vol. 3.

7   (c)   If you answered (a) or (b) read paragraph 2 on p.
            88 of Vol. 3.

8   (b)   You cannot fly a holding pattern on an NDB unless
            you fully understand this question. Therefore if
            you answered (a) or (c) read HOLDING PATTERNS,
            pp. 13-16 in Vol. 3, and study Fig. 2.

9   (b)   While an EAT is rarely given by the Air Traffic
            Control Service there are occasions when it be-
            comes necessary and then there must be no mis-
            understanding the meaning of the term. If you
            answered (a) or (c) read paragraph 2, p. 89-90
            in Vol. 3.

10   (a)   On the basis that the Radio Compass needle always
            points towards the NDB even when this is behind
            the aircraft it should not be difficult to determine
            the direction of drift by imagining the position of
            the beacon. If you answered (b) or (c) read
            FLYING OUTBOUND FROM A BEACON, p. 83
            of Vol. 3, study Fig. 32 and imagine the effect on
            the Radio Compass needle should the top aircraft
            drift to the right. The reading would increase
            and so reproduce this question.

11   (c)   Whether or not the aircraft is working a radio
            facility of any kind whenever it is flying above
            Transition Altitude or Level the Standard Alti-
            meter Setting must be used. If you answered
            (a) or (b) read ALTIMETER SETTING PROCE-
            DURE on pp. 19-20 in Vol. 3.

12   (c)   After an overshoot following an instrument
            approach there may be high ground/obstructions
            to avoid and these are noted on let-down charts
            individually. For safety purposes there is also
            a minimum safe altitude taking into account these
            obstructions and this is listed on the chart as
            'above sea level' or in other words QNH. An
            example of this is the note on the Stansted NDB
            chart illustrated on p. 92 of Vol. 3 where pilots

are warned to maintain 2500 ft (QNH) and contact ATC when for any reason the Sampford Fan Marker cannot be received.

13 (c) If you answered (a) or (b) read HOMING TO THE BEACON on pp. 81-83 in Vol. 3, and study Fig. 31.

14 (a) If you answered (b) or (c) read FLYING OUTBOUND FROM A BEACON, pp. 83-85 in Vol. 3, and study Fig. 32.

15 (a) Answer (b) cannot be correct because a QDR TO is a contradiction in terms and so is alternative (c). If you selected either of these answers read ORIENTATION USING VOR on p. 102 of Vol. 3.

16 (c) If you are drifting to Port the deviation needle will signal FLY RIGHT, therefore answer (a) is incorrect. To read 010° FROM the aircraft would have to be on the other side of the VOR beacon. If you answered (a) or (b), study Fig. 37 on p. 99 but if you are still in doubt read the second and third paragraphs on p. 98 of Vol. 3.

17 (a) Provided the TO-FROM indicator has been set correctly, i.e. showing TO while flying to the VOR beacon and FROM when heading away, the deviation needle will always give corrective signals. In this case the aircraft has approached the beacon with the OBS set on QDM 170° TO. On overflying the beacon the instrument will display OBS 170° FROM when the deviation needle will continue to provide correct 'Fly left/Fly right' information. If you answered (b) or (c) read OMNI-BEARING INDICATOR, pp. 96-100, and study Fig. 37 in Vol. 3. If the top aircraft were to drift to the left the needle would move to the right.

18 (c) If you answered (a) or (b) study Fig. 39 on p. 104 of Vol. 3, but imagine that instead of turning onto 090° you continue on your present heading of 200°. On reaching Radial 270° the deviation needle

would swing in to the centre, then move away to
the left (as seen by the pilot). There is a misprint
in the table that forms part of Fig. 38 (up to the
1972 edition). The information given is correct
when the TO-FROM indicator is reading TO.

19   (b)   Answer (a) would be correct for ILS. If you
             selected (a) or (c) read paragraph 4 of HOMING
             TO THE BEACON on p. 102 of Vol. 3.

20   (c)   When the VOR beacon is off the air the 'OFF' flag
             will appear but unlike the situation described in
             this question the deviation needle will centre.
             Nav. receiver failure may reproduce various indi-
             cations depending on the nature of the fault but full
             deflection of the needle with the 'OFF' flag showing
             is unlikely to be one of these. In most instruments
             the TO-FROM indicator is combined with the 'OFF'
             flag (sometimes called the NO SIGNAL flag) and
             when the aircraft departs from the radial set on the
             OBS by 80° or more this will appear until the air-
             craft has flown to within 80° or so of the radial.
             This is mentioned in paragraph 3, p. 105, Vol. 3.

21   (b)   If you answered (a) or (c) read the note at the
             start of AIR EXERCISE, bottom of p. 101, Vol. 3.
             When you know the accuracy limits in degrees the
             question may be solved by applying the 1-IN-60
             Rule.

22   (a)   A feature of most multi-purpose instruments is
             that only the relevant indications operate when a
             particular facility is selected. For example when
             a combined VOR/ILS indicator is being used on a
             VOR frequency the Glidscope needle will remain
             inoperative in the central position. Likewise
             when an ILS frequency is selected the OBS has no
             effect on the deviation needle which has now be-
             come the LOCALIZER needle. If you answered
             (b) or (c) study Fig. 56 on p. 162 in Vol. 3. This
             shows that the OBS and its related Bearing Scale
             are for VOR purposes only.

23   (a)   If you answered (b) or (c) read HOMING TO AN
             AIRFIELD on p. 61 of Vol. 3, and study Fig. 22.

24   (b)   If you answered (a) or (c) read PPI CONTINUOUS
             DESCENT on p. 149 of Vol. 3.

25   (b)   If you answered (a) or (c) read SUMMARY OF
             RADAR APPROACHES, bottom of p. 150, Vol. 3.

26   (b)   If you answered (a) or (c) read ASSOCIATED
             AIRBORNE EQUIPMENT, from the bottom of
             p. 156, Vol. 3, and study Figs. 53 and 54.

27   (c)   Unlike VOR there is no TO-FROM indicator in
             ILS, therefore localizer signals (i.e. Fly Left-
             Fly Right) are not corrective when the aircraft is
             on a reciprocal heading to the runway QDM. While
             this could be confusing the situation is clarified by
             having a blue and yellow sector marked on the
             instrument which relates to the blue and yellow
             sides of the runway which are always right and left
             of centre line when heading in on the approach. If
             you answered (a) or (b) read from "This instru-
             ment, which forms the . . ." to the end of the para-
             graph on p. 158 of Vol. 3 and study Fig. 53.

28   (a)   Since the Glide Path is beamed at an angle back-
             wards from the runway threshold it follows that
             the greater the distance from the runway the
             higher will be the 3° glide path. An aircraft
             approaching the runway at the correct height will
             remain below the Glide Path, usually until reach-
             ing the Outer Marker Beacon when the associated
             needle will change from 'Fly-up' to 'Central'
             indicating 'On the Glide Path'. If you answered
             (b) or (c) read from No. 6 under the heading THE
             ILS APPROACH on p. 168 of Vol. 3 and study
             Fig. 55.

29   (c)   If you answered (a) or (b) read ASSOCIATED
             AIRBORNE EQUIPMENT on pp. 163-64 of Vol. 3,
             also study Figs. 55 and 57.

30   (a)   Remember that both needles give signals in the
             corrective sense. If you answered (b) or (c),
             study Figs. 53 and 55.

31   (a)   Remember that both needles give signals in the
             corrective sense. If you answered (b) or (c)
             study Figs. 53 and 55.

32   (b)   The Quadrantal Rule is for the purpose of allowing
             pilots to maintain their own height separation
             while flying outside controlled airspace. If you
             answered (a) or (c) read the last paragraph on p.
             175 of Vol. 3 and study the pull-out radio-nav.
             chart (after p. 178 in Vol. 3). AMBER 25 Airway,
             running North-South between Brecon VOR and
             Ormskirk VOR shows EVEN — running North
             and — ODD flying South. These refer to the
             Flight Levels.

33   (c)   If you answered (a) of (b) read FAN MARKERS
             on p. 78 of Vol. 3, and study Fig. 29.

34   (a)   Distance Measuring Equipment means what it says
             but unfortunately this remarkable aid can only
             measure the distance between the beacon and the
             aircraft in a straight line, i.e. air to ground and
             not ground position to beacon. If you answered
             (b) or (c) read DESCRIPTION on pp. 109-111 and
             study Fig. 40.

35   (c)   Some VHF transmitters are of very high power
             but even these rely entirely upon 'Line-of-Sight'
             reception. In this respect VHF transmission is
             rather similar to a light beam. If you answered
             (a) or (b) read FREQUENCY BANDS, pp. 28-31
             of Vol. 3, also study Figs. 7, 8 and 9.

25
90
175